SASSY LIPS

FEARLESS QUEENS

Ignite Your Entrepreneurial Spirit
and Unleash Your Greatest Potential

AROHA RIPLEY

Sassy Lips, Fearless Queens:
Ignite your entrepreneurial spirit and unleash your greatest potential
Aroha Ripley

First published in Australia © 2023 Aroha Ripley
aroharipley.com

ISBN 978-0-6458793-0-8

Cover design: Aroha Ripley, Muhammad Umar Nawaz, Beckon Creative
Editor: Anne Hamilton
Interior typeset & design: Beckon Creative, Aroha Ripley

The author asserts the moral right to be identified as the author of this work.

 A catalogue record for this book is available from the National Library of Australia

SASSY LIPS

FEARLESS QUEENS

Ignite Your Entrepreneurial Spirit and Unleash Your Greatest Potential

AROHA RIPLEY

ENDORSEMENTS

Open up *Sassy Lips, Fearless Queens* by Aroha Ripley and feel a wave of 'I-CAN-DO-IT' hit you. Embark on this transformative journey that empowers you to reclaim your dreams with a fearless passion to pursue your life's desires.

Marie-France Garon,
Health and Wellness Coach

Aroha's message reminds us that empowerment is not just a word, but a journey of resilience, and this book, *Sassy Lips, Fearless Queens*, is a guiding light for anyone seeking to conquer obstacles and find their own path to empowerment.

Rauhena Chase,
Founder of Rauhena Chase Commercial Real Estate

Reading *Sassy Lips, Fearless Queens*, it's a book you can't put down once you start reading from the first page to the last. It is a well-written book by Aroha Ripley and is enriched with an interwoven tapestry of ups and downs and ins and outs that has you on the edge of your seat until the final word. A must-read for anyone who wants clarity in their lives where there is uncertainty as this book arms you with the tools you need to tackle your past, present, and future. Bestseller in my opinion.

Tina Raston,
Proofreader and mother of two sons

Sassy Lips, Fearless Queens tells of the author's personal struggle as a child and then as an adult for her existence to be acknowledged, identified, and validated. Her story is authentic, riveting, powerful, and one of survival. Although written for sassy queens, it will resonate with all people. President Te Korowai Aroha The author is like the legendary Phoenix, 'she rose from the ashes and was renewed' And from the Bible, Isaiah 61:3 To bestow on them a crown of beauty instead of ashes The oil of Joy instead of mourning, and a garment of praise instead of a spirit of despair. Arise Fearless Queen and take a bow!

Mary Bartlett Johnston,
President Te Korowai Aroha, *Funeral Director, Postvention Suicide Counselor*

Aroha is not just talk; she lives the walk. Sharing her journey of overcoming obstacles and realizing her potential in *Sassy Lips, Fearless Queens* is a passionate encouragement that your life has a purpose, and you were meant to flourish as the person you were created to be.

Tania Porter,
student naturopath and mother of five

Sassy Lips, Fearless Queens is an inspiring book with many great lessons. A powerful read about overcoming your fears and pursuing your dreams. *Sassy Lips, Fearless Queens* is a roadmap to unleashing your full potential.

Rebecca Raston,
Founder of Raston Collection

Infused with hard-won wisdom Aroha Ripley's *Sassy Lips, Fearless Queens* is an invitation, in the face of fear, to be Wildly, Passionately, Outrageously devoted to life. Kindnesses, Grief, Despair, and especially Love- the large and small signatures are all here, Recognizable, Heartbreaking, Confirming, and extremely Encouraging. I held this profound and courageous book to my heart... it brought me "Confidence" to trust my "Feminine Instincts" and gave me "Permission" to embrace my "Inner Queen".

Sommer May Lee

If you're seeking inspiration and a push to pursue your dreams, look no further than *Sassy Lips, Fearless Queens*. Aroha Ripley speaks to the heart and soul, delivering a powerful message of resilience and success.

Erene Edera,
Founder of Mykokomoment

CONTENTS

	Foreword	13
	Dedication	17
	Introduction	21
PART ONE	**EMPOWER MY QUEENS**	**27**
Chapter 1	**Life Seems So Unfair:** *The Power of Letting Go, My Queen*	29
Chapter 2	**Crafting a Queen's Mindset:** *Rebuilding and Mastering the Power of Your Mind*	49
Chapter 3	**Conquering Adversity Like A Queen:** *Unleashing the Power of a Fearless Queen*	59
Chapter 4	**Reign Like A Queen:** *Embrace Life with Sass and Passion*	69

PART TWO	**EQUIPPING MY QUEENS**	**81**
Chapter 5	**Equip and Conquer:** Empowering Fierce Queens with the Right Tools and Resources	83
Chapter 6	**From Vision to Reality:** Building Unstoppable Empires with a Queen's Foundation	93
Chapter 7	**Slay Queen Supreme:** Conquer and Seize Every Fabulous Opportunity	103
PART THREE	**EVOLVE, MY QUEENS**	**113**
Chapter 8	**Get Ready to Embrace Change:** Like Sassy Lips and Fearless Queens	115
Chapter 9	**Queen's Guide:** Unleashing Lasting Transformation Like a Queen!	125
Chapter 10	**Queens Unleashed:** Reigning with Sass and Unstoppable Commitment to Continuous Growth	135

PART FOUR	ENTHRONE MY QUEENS	145
Chapter 11	**Owning Your Throne:** *Sassy Lips Fearless Queen Edition:* Building Your Business	147
Chapter 12	**Empire Building Allies:** Forging Strong Partnerships with Manufacturers	175
Chapter 13	**Building Powerful Alliances:** Reaching Out to Influencers and Corporate Partners	181
Chapter 14	**A Letter to My Queen**	189
Chapter 15	**The Essence of Sassy Lips, Fearless Queen**	195
Chapter 16	**The Royal Roadmap:** Time for Sassy Empowerment	201
Chapter 17	**Handy Tools and Resources:** Building Your QUEENdom	207

APPENDICES		
	A Special Invitation for My Queen	223
	My Prayer for My Sassy Lips, Fearless Queen	227
	About the Author	231
	Acknowledgments	233
	Want to Know More?	237

FOREWORD

Tracy M. Wilson

WHO SAID YOU CAN'T REIGN LIKE A QUEEN?

"Enough is enough!" This rallying cry is more than just an emphatic statement — it's a call to action, a catalyst for transformation. Just like Aroha Ripley outlines in the chapters that follow, sometimes life pushes us to a point where standing still is no longer an option.

How did we get here? What have we internalized that has been holding us back? Is it self-doubt, fear of failure, or the societal norms that box you into specific roles? The chapters that follow will help you craft a Queen's mindset, breaking through those barriers with a sledgehammer of fearless sass.

Sassy Lips

The societal norms we're told to conform to are not our destiny. The challenges and constraints we face — whether it's early motherhood or the corporate glass ceiling—are not limitations but the very crucibles in which our Queen's essence is forged. *Sassy Lips, Fearless Queens* is aimed at liberating not just your career, but your very essence.

But let's not gloss over it: our world is in flux. In the grand tapestry of history, women are stitching their narratives like never before. I'm not just talking about the boardroom but every facet of life. If Forbes is calling this the "Golden Age for Women Entrepreneurs," then books like *Sassy Lips, Fearless Queens* are the golden scrolls. They are more than just words on a page; they are the catalysts for action, the blueprints for building empires, and the choruses in a growing anthem of female empowerment. Aroha does an exceptional job capturing this ethos in her book. She speaks directly to you, enveloping you in a conversational tone that makes you feel like a confidante.

There's a passage where Aroha talks about "letting go," a topic so emotionally charged and universally experienced that it resonates with each of us. This approach, blended with Aroha's insights, creates a multi-dimensional roadmap to "thrivability" — a term I love!

While diving into these chapters, you'll quickly realize that the wisdom encapsulated here is not just a product of individual effort. This book stands as a testament to the transformative power of community and collective guidance. It's more than just one woman's perspective; it's a synthesis of voices that encourages all of us to uplift one another.

So why should you invest your time and energy into these pages? Because in an era of unprecedented chaos, uncertainty, and change, grounding yourself in an authentic, unshakeable identity is more important than ever. *Sassy Lips, Fearless Queens* is more than a book; it's a lifeline.

It's your turn now. Your turn to delve deep into the transformative journey that Aroha has crafted for you. Your turn to slay, to reign, and to build an empire of your own design.

Who said you can't reign like a queen? Welcome to your coronation.

Your journey begins now.

Tracy M. Wilson
Best-selling author of The She Myth: Redefining Women in Business, *coach, and host of the* Unlocked *podcast*

DEDICATION

This book is a passionate dedication to the women who've carried doubts about their rightful claim to success, those who've hesitated to chase their dreams due to feelings of unworthiness. Let these pages be a resounding call to action, igniting a fire within you to embark on a soul-stirring expedition of self-discovery. May you dig deep, unearthing the priceless essence of your being and unapologetically acknowledging your inherent worth. Embrace the awe-inspiring array of life's possibilities waiting for you, for they are yours to claim.

In loving memory of my dear mother, Hannah Wairoa Williams, and in tribute to my cherished nannies, Mareti Williams and Charlotte Morehu. Your indelible influence has established the bedrock of strength and independence within me, emphasizing the significance of walking with integrity and acting with love, and fearlessly pursuing the core values of life — family and the profound love of Jesus.

Sassy Lips

In loving tribute to my dear sister, Ruth, affectionately known as "Mama Ruth." Your recent departure from this earthly realm has left a significant void within us. Your incredible and affectionate nature and love as a sister remains etched in my heart. Your steadfast love and genuine concern for the happiness of those around you has touched us deeply and shone as a guiding beacon. Your dreams and ambitions my beautiful sister will forever weave into the fabric of my own journey. Forever in my heart, my beloved sister, till we meet again in the loving arms of Jesus.

My dearest sisters, Margie, Evie, and Daystar, no matter the miles that separate us or the differences in our personalities, our sisterly bond and love are constants that will forever unite us, love you.

To my beautiful daughter Janaya, As I write these words, my heart swells with pride and gratitude for the wonderful woman you've become. Your kindness, your unwavering determination, and the love you carry within you – they fill my days with such joy. I wanted to take a moment to express my gratitude for simply being you — for our heart-to-heart conversations, your unwavering support, and the warmth that radiates from your very being.

As you continue on your journey, always remember that you hold immense potential within you. Your dreams and aspirations are worth chasing, and I have no doubt that you'll achieve greatness. You are a true blessing, my beloved daughter, and I cherish every moment we share. Know that my love for you knows no bounds.

Ema and Nina, our cherished daughters-in-law, we are truly blessed to have you, both in our lives, showering us with your boundless love. Your constant support and affection bring an extra dose of happiness to the beautiful fabric of our family. Seeing your passion for what you do and your dedication to family warms our hearts and serves as a great inspiration. We love you both.

And finally to our beloved and future mokopunas, Eva, Isla, Wynter, and Willow, and our beautiful Melody always in our hearts. My darlings, life is like this incredible adventure just waiting for you, and guess what? You've got all the tools you need to make it absolutely extraordinary. Dream big, my mokopunas, and go after those dreams with all your heart. As you continue to grow, always remember that you're walking in the footsteps of remarkable women who came before you. You're carrying forward their legacy, and it's a pretty remarkable one. Love you all

Nanny xx

INTRODUCTION

Dear esteemed reader, I'd like to take a moment to introduce myself. *Kia ora*, I'm Aroha Ripley. I am of Māori descent with indigenous heritage. I grew up in the picturesque landscapes of Hawera and the small town of Levin, nestled in Aotearoa, New Zealand. These days, I've made my home in sunny Brisbane, Australia. My area of expertise lies in the realm of business coaching, mentoring, and creative talent. I want to speak to you from the depths of my heart. If you have ever felt the painful sting of hurtful words like "You're not good enough," or "You'll never amount to anything; you're useless," if you've been told to zip it, diminished, or forced into silence by the insecurities of others, I understand your pain. But let me tell you, it's time to rise above and reclaim your power. *Sassy Lips, Fearless Queens* was written specifically for you, the woman who has felt beaten down and lost, and is questioning her purpose in life. May this book be your guiding light and a source of

Sassy Lips

hope and inspiration. Within these pages, I share my personal journey of triumph over adversity, and I promise you that there is a way out, a way to turn everything around for the better.

Sassy Lips, Fearless Queens is not just a catchy phrase — it holds a profound meaning. It represents the boldness to express yourself unapologetically and to speak your truth with confidence. It embodies the strength and courage to rise above any obstacle and conquer your fears and doubts. The purpose of this book is to ignite the fire within you, to help you overcome challenges, and to live a life filled with purpose and authenticity. I want you to know that you have the power within you to break free from limitations and embrace your true potential.

In writing this book, my aim is to create a community of empowered women where we celebrate and uplift one another. It is a place where you can find the courage to step into your power, break free from societal expectations, fully embrace your unique gifts and talents, and ignite your entrepreneurial spirit. Consider this book your guide, a roadmap that will lead you towards fulfilling your God-given purpose. I want you to know that your dreams are valid and that you are deserving of an extraordinary life.

With sincerity and warmth, I invite you to embrace your quirks, your vibrant personality, and all the qualities that make you who you are. Be unapologetically yourself, and know that you are enough. Together, let's embark on a journey of self-discovery where you can unleash your authentic self, your inner queen, and make a positive impact in the world, and reach your greatest potential. Let the pages of *Sassy Lips, Fearless Queens* be a source of inspiration and motivation, igniting the fire within you to pursue your dreams and live life to the fullest.

From the bottom of my heart, I want you to know that I believe in you. You have the strength and resilience to overcome any obstacle that comes your way. Trust in yourself, and let the fearless queen within you shine brightly. This is your time to embrace your true worth and create a life that is filled with love, joy, and fulfillment. Together, let's embark on this heartfelt journey of self-discovery and celebrate the incredible woman that you are destined to become.

With deep affection that knows no bounds, I stand before you as your unwavering Queen of Sass and Fearlessness,

Aroha xx

Disclaimer: My personal story includes elements of sexual abuse, violence, and attempted suicide that might not be suitable for readers and may trigger past or existing traumas. Readers who may be sensitive to these elements should take note. Seek professional help where needed. If you are in Australia, please call 1800 RESPECT, the National Domestic Family and Sexual Violence Counseling Service.

Sassy Lips

Sassy Lips
speak the language of confidence
~ while ~
Fearless Queens
walk the path of success.

PART ONE

EMPOWER *my* QUEENS

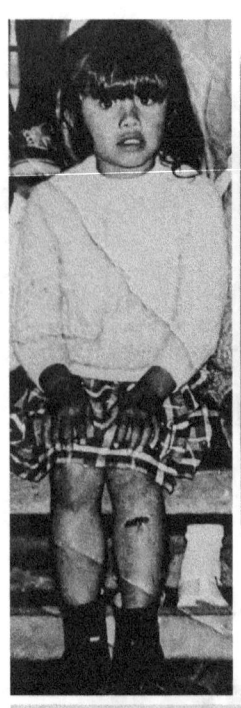
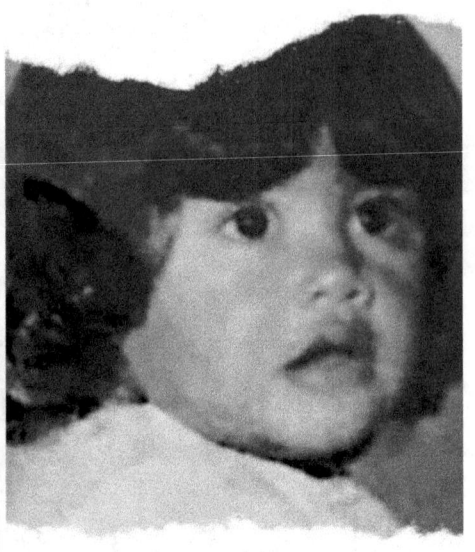

BEHIND CLOSED DOORS
A STORY OF HOPE

LIFE SEEMS SO UNFAIR

THE POWER OF LETTING GO, My Queen

Ladies, it's time to gather 'round, for I'm about to unleash my personal tale of triumph, resilience, and the art of conquering every challenge that came my way, and the importance of letting go of past hurts. So grab your crowns and fasten your seatbelts, because this story is about to take you on an exhilarating journey of strength and determination.

Picture this: A queen facing the world head-on, unyielding in the face of adversity. That queen is me. Throughout my life, I've encountered hurdles that would make some people crumble. But guess what? I didn't just survive; I thrived. With sass as my armor and confidence as my shield, I pushed forward with unwavering resolve.

Challenges? Oh, I've had my fair share. From the darkest pits of self-doubt to the treacherous twists of fate, life tested me in ways that would make lesser mortals shudder. But did I back down? Absolutely not. I embraced those challenges, stared them down, and said, "Bring it on!"

My queens, the secret lies in the way we perceive obstacles. While others may view them as insurmountable walls, I now see them as mere stepping stones on the path to greatness. Each trial became an opportunity to prove my courage, to rise above the chaos, and to show the world what a true queen is capable of.

But rising above isn't just about conquering external forces; it starts from within. I harnessed the power of self-belief, turning it into a force that could move mountains. I learned to trust in my abilities, to silence the voices of doubt, and to tap into the wellspring of strength that resides within every queen.

Sassy Lips

Sure, there were moments when the weight of the world threatened to break me. But I refused to let it. I stood tall, shoulders back, and chin held high, because that's what queens do. We face our challenges with a grace that can only come from knowing our worth and our power.

You see, I couldn't have done it without my personal relationship with Jesus, which is what helped me get through life's obstacles. It isn't just a spiritual connection; it's a source of empowerment. It's about recognizing that you are a daughter of the King, a queen in your own right, and that you possess a divine spark within you. Through Jesus, you tap into a reservoir of love, grace, and courage that knows no bounds.

As I share my tale of trials and triumphs, let it serve as a reminder that you too possess the resilience, the audacity, and the unwavering spirit of a true queen. Life may throw curveballs, but remember this: you have the power to rise above, to conquer, and to reign supreme. It's time to buckle in, my queens, as I begin to share my story.

Listen up, my magnificent queens, because I've got a tale to tell that will stir your souls and touch the deepest fibers of your being. It's time to set aside the sass for a moment and embrace the gravity of my personal story, for there are chapters that demand our undivided attention. In this chapter, I want to take you back to the beginning, my queens, to a time when everything seemed bleak, the challenges ahead seemed insurmountable, and life seemed so unfair. This is the story of my personal journey, where I emerged from years of enduring the darkest moments at a time when adversity seemed to surround me from all directions. Let me introduce myself and give you a glimpse into my life during those trying times. I'll share the setbacks I faced, the personal struggles that weighed me down, and the doubts that clouded my mind. It was during this period that I felt the weight of the world on my shoulders, unsure of how to navigate the storms that raged around me.

In the depths of my journey, I stumbled upon a cherished photo, a portal to the past that revealed more than just captured memories. As I held it in my hands, my heart trembled, for the words inscribed on the back struck a chord so deep within me. "Tossed to and fro, but God will be her Father, and she shall know Him." These words echoed with the weight of my mother's challenges, the fractures in our relationship, and the love she struggled to give me. It was a revelation that pierced through the layers of our shared history, shedding light on the complexities that shaped our bond.

But let me take you even further back, my queens, to a time when the world seemed relentlessly bleak, and the weight of the challenges before me threatened to crush my spirit. Life felt unfair, the path ahead appeared insurmountable, and adversity lurked around every corner. It was in those dark moments that I emerged, battered but unbroken, from the depths of my own personal abyss. The storms raged, but I refused to be swept away.

As I recount my story, we'll dive deep into the depths of the adversity I encountered. It wasn't just a single challenge; it was a series of setbacks that tested my resilience and determination. From personal losses to rejection and financial hardship, each blow seemed to push me further into a state of despair. But little did I know that these trials would be the catalyst for a profound transformation.

It's never easy to hear those painful words from your own mother. "You will never become anything; you are useless, and no one will want you." The continuous echo of negative words from your parents demoralizes any confidence or hope in a child's feeling of being loved or accepted. What does that do to your moral development as a child, let alone when you become an adult?

As a child, I experienced years of instability, constantly being shuffled between different homes. Just when I would start to settle in with a new family, I would be uprooted and brought back home. It was clear that I didn't fit in with my own family, and that fact was reinforced every time I was taken away.

My anger grew with each upheaval, and I ended up running away countless times, desperate to escape the toxic environment I was in. This cycle of instability repeated itself for many years.

One fateful day, a revelation unfolded as my mother summoned the courage to share a long-held secret — a truth I had never known before. My heart grew heavy as my mother's words reverberated through the room, each syllable laden with vulnerability.

"Aroha," she whispered, her voice trembling, "I named you Aroha, which means *love* in our Māori language. But I couldn't offer you the love you deserved." With bated breath, I continued to listen as her story unfolded, revealing a painful truth that shattered my world — "I did not want you at birth; you were a girl and not the son I had longed for." At that moment, the pieces of our fractured bond fell into place, and the walls of distance and detachment finally made sense. Tears welled up in my eyes as my mother uttered those words, her voice laced with regret. "I prayed for you," she confessed, "and asked God to protect you and grant you the love you deserved because I couldn't provide it." At that moment, the truth hit me like a tidal wave, crashing against the shores of my heart. Sometimes, the truth hurts. How does one handle such a profound rejection? I can tell you, it plays havoc with your mindset, leaving you searching for answers in the midst of the pain.

The haunting feeling of being unwanted and unaccepted is a relentless companion, gnawing at your soul, whether you're a vulnerable child or a grown adult. It's a turbulent storm that ravages your mind, plunging you into a maddening abyss of despair. In the darkest depths of my existence, I found myself grappling with thoughts that echoed with anguish. There were moments when the heaviness of it all made me question my very existence, and the overwhelming desire to fade away consumed my every thought.

To navigate this treacherous terrain, I became a master of disguises, an actor in the tragic theatre of life. I mastered the art of donning a deceiving smile, even as my heart crumbled in silent agony. I learned the skill of uttering the words society wanted to hear, diverting attention from the searing pain that simmered within.

But beneath the façade, I carefully hid my shattered fragments of hurt and rage, locking them away in the deepest recesses of my being, shielding them from prying eyes.

My smile became a battlefield, a desperate defense mechanism erected to shield my vulnerability from a callous world. It was both my fortress and my prison, for within its fragile embrace, I sought solace while silently screaming for release.

How could the seeds of my potential ever find the light they needed to sprout and grow, when the searing heat of disbelief etched its painful scars into the very core of who I was? It was inflicted by the one I held closest to my heart, adding an extra layer of hurt to the wounds I carried.

Growing up, I would often gaze at other families with a longing in my heart, yearning to be a part of their warmth and belonging, even to the point of jealousy. I felt so adrift, wondering where I truly fit in. It was a painful realization that the love of a parent is not automatically guaranteed, simply by virtue of being their child. If you were fortunate enough to experience such unconditional love from your earliest days, consider yourself truly blessed. Don't ever take it for granted.

As a child, my desperation to be accepted and loved was about to lead me down a path I could never have imagined. Little did I know that a nightmare was lurking just around the corner, waiting to unfold its dark grasp on my life.

Sadly, I became a victim of sexual abuse, enduring it from childhood through my teenage years. This perpetrator was a well-known person to the family who hid behind his authority as a self-proclaimed pastor in a small village. Hear me, there are genuinely remarkable individuals who embody the love of Jesus Christ and serve as true ambassadors of His teachings. Their actions align harmoniously with their words, and the evidence of God's love shines brightly through the fruits they bear. A perpetrator knows exactly how to groom their victims by using the right words and façade. It felt as though I was being led to the slaughter, like a vulnerable lamb, oblivious to the imminent danger lurking just around the corner.

That's precisely why, even to this day, I firmly stand by the belief that actions speak louder than words alone.

What is even more painful is when you have opened your soul to a beloved family member only for them to sweep it under the carpet and also blame you for the sexual predator's repulsive actions. They knew exactly what he was doing, yet they made a deliberate choice to look the other way and do nothing about it.

The anger that surged within me was overpowering, and thoughts of seeking revenge consumed my mind. The hatred I felt was overwhelming, and it made me physically sick. Throughout my earlier years, I had hidden my shame and suffered in silence, blaming myself for allowing the abuse to happen. Yet, it was perpetrated by someone I had once trusted. I was just a child, a teenager who had nowhere to turn. Behind my smile, I concealed the depths of my pain, but the wound grew so deep that it led me to attempt suicide. I'm not proud of that moment, but the weight of guilt, shame, and the tormenting voices in my head became unbearable. In my mind, I believed that I would be better off not existing anymore. But by the grace of God, it wasn't my time to leave this earth. There was a purpose for me, a purpose I had yet to discover amidst all the turmoil.

In a world that often encourages us to bury painful truths beneath a façade, I made a bold choice to defy the norm. It took every ounce of courage within me, unleashing a torrent of emotions that had been building within me. It was an overwhelming journey, both physically and emotionally, but I mustered the strength to break my silence. I knew that carrying the weight of this secret had consumed me for far too long. Its damage had taken its toll on my well-being, and I reached a pivotal moment where I recognized the urgent need to unshackle myself from its suffocating grip.

A new chapter in my life was on the horizon, but it didn't guarantee smooth sailing or a bed of roses. In fact, quite the opposite was true.

The relationship with my mother reached new depths of deterioration. Our communication dwindled to almost nothing, leaving us as mere strangers, crossing paths without truly connecting. The words she lashed out with carried a venomous sting, piercing deep into the core of my being. Their echoes resonated relentlessly within me, a constant reminder of my perceived worthlessness. It seemed that no matter how hard I tried, I remained trapped in an unending cycle, desperately yearning for her love and approval — a battle that proved futile, and impossible to conquer. It felt as if she held the reins of my life, controlling my every step, while I clung to her words as irrefutable truth.

Without her validation, my dreams and aspirations appeared feeble, my sense of identity diminished, and my self-worth shattered into countless fragmented pieces.

I found myself engulfed in an insatiable curiosity, tormented by relentless questions that gnawed at the core of my being. Why was I the target of such unrelenting mistreatment from those who were meant to shield and cherish me? What had I done to deserve this heart-wrenching treatment? The quest for truth led me down a treacherous path, filled with uncertainty and the looming fear of uncovering painful realities. Accepting the possibility that the answers I yearned for might forever elude me was a bitter pill to swallow, saturating my world with a profound sense of loss. In that pivotal moment, I stood at a crossroads, faced with a daunting choice: to wage a fierce battle for a better existence or to succumb and escape from the suffocating darkness that enveloped me.

At the age of 15, I made the decision to drop out of school and leave home. I immediately sought work and found a place to board, eager to distance myself from my home environment. It was up to me to forge my own path in life, and I knew it wouldn't be easy. There were times when I couldn't afford to eat, resorting to eating scraps off the plates as a kitchen hand. Pride prevented me from asking for help; I wanted to prove that I could be independent. I took on various jobs, including being a kitchen hand, waitress, cleaner, factory worker, vegetable picker, and even working in shearing sheds as a rousie. I did whatever it took to pay my board and stay away from home.

But each day, the scars of my trauma deepened, etching their painful imprints upon my fragile being. They became the shackles that bound me, chaining me to a desolate path of self-doubt, diminished self-worth, and relentless mistrust. The weight of my struggles cast me into the abyss of despair, where the demons of depression, anxiety, and self-harm lurked, their haunting whispers echoing through the corridors of my tormented mind.

I spent much time trying to figure out what my next steps were, still struggling to even find them. I was avoiding the truth of what was really going on, which created even more turmoil within. I was desperate to find peace, and I knew it was time to confront the truths of my past head-on. I had to learn to refuse any concept of victimhood that would steal the peace and stop me from moving forward.

If I wanted to get better, I needed to seek the right help, let the walls of pride come down, and step out of the default position of victimhood. Was I up for the challenge? No. Was I ready to be vulnerable? No. But I knew, if I kept going on with my emotions and the blame game, I would remain in my world of loneliness, negativity, and hopelessness.

Yet, my story is not a solitary tale of sorrow. It resonates with the struggles and sorrows of countless souls, carrying the weight of their own hidden wounds. Together, we stand at the edge of missed opportunities, our lives obscured by the lingering effects of past trauma and deeply ingrained beliefs. It is a heartbreaking tragedy that so many of us remain oblivious to the beckoning call of our true purpose, entangled in the intricate threads of our past.

In our journey, we often let misfortune define us, hindering our God-given destinies. We carry the weight of shame, guilt, and others' expectations, living a life of frustration and conformity. But it doesn't have to be this way. You have the power to break free, embrace your true self, and step into a life of purpose and fulfillment. Let go of past burdens, forgive yourself, and surround yourself with uplifting people. Trust in the divine plan for you and have faith in your ability to create a life that surpasses your wildest dreams. It's time to shine brightly and embark on the incredible adventure of self-discovery and transformation.

As I reflect on the path I have walked, I can't deny that it hasn't always been easy, and it feels like life has been so unfair. Along the way, I encountered numerous obstacles that threatened to derail me, faced setbacks that left me questioning my abilities, and weathered storms that tested the very core of my being. Yet, through it all, there was an unwavering fire within me — a flame that refused to be extinguished.

In those moments of struggle, I made a choice to embrace the challenges as opportunities for growth, to view setbacks as stepping stones towards something greater, and to transform adversity into fuel for my journey. It was this choice, rooted in the depths of my being, that allowed me to rise above the trials that came my way.

The fire within me burned brighter with each hurdle I conquered. It ignited a determination that propelled me forward, even when the path seemed uncertain and the odds were stacked against me. I refused to let the setbacks define me or hold me back. Instead, I used them as catalysts for personal transformation and as reminders of the strength I possessed within.

Sassy Lips

There were moments when the flames flickered when doubt and fatigue threatened to dim their glow. But I held on, drawing strength from the flickering embers, and re-igniting the fire with unwavering belief in my abilities. I reminded myself of the dreams that fueled my passion, the purpose that resonated in my heart, and the knowledge that I had come too far to give up.

It was in those challenging times that I discovered my true strength — the strength to persevere, to adapt, and to find hidden opportunities within adversity. I learned that setbacks were not signs of failure but invitations to grow and evolve. I embraced the lessons they taught me, using them as stepping stones to propel me further along my journey.

As I stand here today, I carry the scars of battles fought and won, my queen. They serve as reminders of the resilience I possess and the capacity within me to overcome any obstacle. My journey has shaped me, molded me, and shown me the depths of my own potential.

I hope my story serves as a beacon of hope and inspiration for you, my queen. May it remind you that you, too, have an unyielding fire within you: a fire that can guide you through the darkest moments and propel you towards the opportunities that await. You have the strength to overcome any challenge, the resilience to bounce back from setbacks, and the power to transform adversity into stepping stones on your path to success.

Embrace the fire within you. Let it light the way as you navigate the twists and turns of your own journey. Remember that setbacks are not the end of your story, but merely chapters in a larger narrative. Trust in your ability to rise above, to learn and grow from each experience, and to seize the opportunities that arise.

In the face of adversity, let your fire burn brighter, my queen. Allow it to fuel your determination, ignite your passion, and push you towards the limitless possibilities that await. You are capable of so much more than you realize, and your journey has the power to inspire and impact those around you.

In this beautiful tapestry of life, there are souls who are destined to cross paths with you, my queen, to inspire you, and to illuminate the way forward. These extraordinary individuals possess wisdom and insight that resonate deep within our hearts, gently nudging us towards our true purpose. They are the beacons of light that God places in our lives, guiding us through the darkness, reminding us of our inherent worth, and igniting the spark of hope within us.

I pray that your journey is enriched with such encounters: moments where you connect with souls who see the greatness within you, who believe in

Sassy Lips

your dreams, and who offer unwavering support and guidance. These individuals, be they mentors, friends, or kindred spirits,
will walk alongside you, offering wisdom, encouragement,
and the reassurance that
you are never alone,
my queen.

Release the past, embrace your power.

Fearless Queens know the strength in letting go.

CRAFTING A QUEEN'S MINDSET

chapter 2

REBUILDING AND MASTERING THE POWER OF YOUR MIND

Alright, my queen, we're diving deep into the journey of rebuilding a mother-daughter relationship. It's time to make some serious moves, my queen. Rebuilding requires your precious time, effort, and a whole lot of healing. We're here to create a renewed mindset and to show the world what we're made of. This may not be a flawless bond, but guess what? It marks the beginning of a heartfelt reconciliation between a mother and her daughter. We were both determined to give it our all.

Sure, we knew it wouldn't be a walk in the park. Let's be real; smooth sailing isn't our style. But amidst the chaos, we saw a glimmer of hope for a brighter future. A future where love and empathy bridge the divides that try to tear us apart. And let me tell you, that's a cause worth pouring every bit of our energy into. It's a commitment to unwavering patience and forgiveness, both for ourselves and each other.

We made sincere efforts to let go of the past, but let's be honest — it has a sneaky way of creeping back in, causing more harm than good. I reached a point where I said, "Enough is enough!" I refused to carry any more of that hurt from bygone days. I came to a powerful realization: I might not have all the answers I seek, but you know what? I discovered something truly precious — my own healing. And let me tell you, my queen, that healing became my top priority. It meant keeping certain people at arm's length, whether they were family or friends. My well-being took center stage, and I owned it like a queen.

Now, let's talk about letting go. It's no walk in the park, my fierce soul. It can feel like an uphill battle, dragging those heavy weights off our hearts and souls. But here's the thing: letting go is the start of something truly remarkable. It's about finding that inner peace that brings a sense of serenity to your life. It's about acknowledging that there's a whole freakin' world out

Sassy Lips

there, just waiting for you to embrace it with open arms and slay the game.

One of the biggest challenges I faced on my journey was mastering my mindset. Those voices in my head were overwhelming, constantly filling my mind with self-limiting beliefs and casting shadows of doubt. But guess what? I had a moment where I said, "Hell no, not today!" I embarked on a journey to challenge those self-limiting beliefs and infuse my mind with empowering thoughts. It was like planting seeds of beauty in the garden of my mind, ready to watch them bloom and flourish. It meant kicking toxic old habits and thought patterns to the curb. I was done with the negativity that only held me back.

Every day, I embarked on an intimate and personal journey to confront those negative patterns that had taken hold of my thoughts. I channeled unwavering determination and dove deep into the depths of my own mind. It was like being a badass detective, searching for clues to unravel the truth from the falsehood. I sought professional help, turned to mentors, and dug deep within myself to examine my beliefs. I carefully discerned what was rooted in truth and what was a distorted perception. I let go of what no longer served me and embraced what brought me joy and growth. It was a personal journey of self-discovery and empowerment, paving the way for a more fulfilling life. Let me tell you, it was an eye-opening experience as I started to recognize the triggers and moments when negativity would try to take hold.

Armed with this newfound awareness, I harnessed the power of reframing. Those negative thoughts? They didn't stand a chance against my fierce sass. I deliberately reframed them into positive and affirming statements. But let's be clear, my queen — it wasn't just my strength that fueled this transformation. I found solace and guidance in the Bible, in the words of the Almighty, and in the power of His love.

In those moments of doubt and self-criticism, I turned to the wisdom and promises found within God's Word. I reminded myself of His unconditional love and grace and the epic plan He had for my life. His words became a shield against the negativity, a beacon of light that illuminated my path. With each reframe, the grip of negativity loosened, and I felt a surge of peace and strength envelop me. The power of God's word and love transformed my mindset, infusing it with hope, resilience, and unbreakable faith.

Step by sassy step, I rewrote the narrative of my thoughts. I replaced self-doubt with self-acceptance, fear with courage, and despair with hope. Each positive affirmation, backed by God's word, became a stepping stone toward a healthier and more loving mindset. As I continued on this path,

Sassy Lips

it was like unearthing a hidden treasure chest within the depths of my own soul. Can you even imagine, my queen? I stumbled upon buried dreams, passions, and aspirations that had been overshadowed by self-doubt and the weight of society's expectations.

Through deep introspection and self-reflection, I unearthed these precious gems within me. In the midst of the chaos within my mind, I discovered the power of quieting the noise, the doubts, the expectations, and the opinions of others. Instead, I tuned in to the soft whispers of my own heart. It was a profound shift. It guided me towards a path that felt undeniably authentic and true to the fierce queen I am at my core.

I started painting the most vibrant picture of the life I had always longed for. It was a life infused with purpose, overflowing with joy, love, and an unapologetic sense of authenticity. Each stroke of my brush revealed new hues of happiness and fulfilment. Trust me, it was an awe-inspiring masterpiece in the making, and it continues to evolve with every sassy step I take.

My fierce and fabulous queen, because it's time to unleash your power and conquer the art of letting go. You, my darlings, possess an unstoppable force within you, capable of rising above any challenge, hurt, or negativity that comes your way. So hold your head high, embrace you're freedom, and unleash that inner sass that sets your soul on fire.

You were never meant to be confined by the chains of the past. It's time to break free, my queen, and let go of what no longer serves you. Those toxic relationships, those hurtful memories, and those self-limiting beliefs — they've had their time. It's your turn to soar to new heights, leaving behind anything that dampens your spirit.

I want you to take a moment and bask in the power that resides within you. Feel the fire burning deep in your soul, ready to ignite your path to greatness. Embrace that confidence, that sass, and that unapologetic spirit that sets you apart. You were born to reign, my queen, and nothing — absolutely nothing — can stand in your way.

But here's the secret ingredient to your triumph: it's all in your mindset. You have the power to shape your thoughts, to infuse them with love, and to banish negativity from your kingdom. So, my sassy queen, I challenge you to overcome your mindset with an army of good-loving thoughts.

When doubt creeps in and insecurities try to rear their ugly heads, I want you to combat them with fierce self-acceptance and unwavering self-love. Remind yourself of your worth and of the incredible journey you've embarked upon. Believe in your abilities, your strengths, and your unique beauty. Let those thoughts become your armor, shielding you from the negativity that seeks to bring you down.

And when you encounter hurdles along the way, my queen, remember that they are simply stepping stones on your path to greatness. Embrace them as opportunities for growth and transformation. Rise above the challenges, learn from them, and let them propel you forward.

As you embark on this journey of letting go and creating a new mindset, always hold onto the truth that you are worthy of love, happiness, and all the blessings life has to offer. Trust in your inner strength and embrace the freedom that comes with releasing what no longer serves you. Remember, my queen, you are the ruler of your own destiny, and your reign knows no bounds.

So, my sassy queen, as you navigate the art of letting go, go forth with unyielding confidence, unwavering sass, and an unbreakable spirit. Embrace your power, release those chains, and soar to new heights. The world is yours for the taking, my queen, and I have no doubt that you will reign supreme.

Crafting a **Queen's mindset** is like forging a diamond: it takes **pressure, resilience** and **unwavering belief** to create a mindset that shines with **unbreakable brilliance**

CONQUERING ADVERSITY LIKE A QUEEN

chapter 3

UNLEASHING THE POWER OF A FEARLESS QUEEN

Honestly, navigating the crazy rollercoaster ride of my relationship with my mother was like riding a wild adventure. We faced more twists and turns than I could count, and let me tell you, it was no walk in the park. But here's the deal, my friend: healing and overcoming adversity take time and effort. It's not a quick fix or an overnight magic trick.

But guess what? I've learned that with a whole lot of patience, unyielding resilience, and a hunger to learn from life's crazy lessons, we can make progress like nobody's business. And guess what? You're not alone in this epic journey. There are countless fierce warriors who have battled their own demons and emerged stronger than ever. Their words of wisdom and encouragement are here to guide us as we forge ahead on our path to greatness.

In the time we've got left on this crazy ride, my mother and I experienced a real-life miracle: reconciliation. It was a precious gift that allowed us to mend our shattered relationship and embrace the fierce love that binds us as mother and daughter. Let me tell you, my queen, that through her unwavering support, my mother became my ultimate hype queen, cheering me on to embrace the divine purpose that God has laid on my path. Her words ignited a fire within me, fueling my determination to chase my dreams like a queen. Can you believe it? The person I once thought was my arch-nemesis turned out to be my ride-or-die supporter, pushing me to the top. Our story is a testament to the incredible power of love and forgiveness to transform adversity into something beautiful. My fierce queen: know this, you're not alone on this wild journey. There's a whole squad of support and guidance ready to lift you up and help you conquer whatever life throws your way.

Sassy Lips

When I look back at my own journey of kicking adversity in the face, I'm humbled by the colossal transformation it brought into my life. Adversity has this knack for shaking us to our very core, challenging every belief, value, and priority we hold dear. It's like a cosmic wake-up call that demands our undivided attention and forces us to take a closer look at who the heck we truly are and what truly matters to our fabulous souls. In those moments of struggle, we find ourselves reevaluating our dreams and aspirations, questioning whether they align with our authentic selves.

Adversity becomes the ultimate catalyst for growth and self-discovery, unveiling our hidden strengths and unlocking our potential. It's through the process of navigating through life's twists and turns that we emerge as resilient, wise warriors, armed with a fresh perspective on life that screams, "Bring it on, Universe!" Life sure has a sneaky way of throwing challenges our way, doesn't it? But guess what? We're not going to back down. In the face of tough times, we're going to slay like the queen we are. We'll harness the power of adversity like a queen, using it as a springboard for our personal growth and transformation. Instead of letting the tough stuff drag us down, we're going to embrace it like a spicy ingredient that adds flavor to our fabulous lives. Adversity is our secret sauce, teaching us valuable lessons, unlocking hidden strengths, and revealing new dimensions of our awesomeness. By embracing adversity, we transform it into a force that propels us forward, allowing us to rise above any obstacle and become the fierce, unstoppable beings we were meant to be.

Let's be real, my queen. Life can be a wild and wacky ride, with unexpected curveballs flying at us left and right. But you know what? We're adaptable like chameleons, ready to face whatever comes our way. We might stumble and fall, but we'll always rise back up, dust off our fabulous selves, and rock those challenges like nobody's business. Adversity teaches us the art of flexibility and the importance of embracing change. It might not always be comfortable, but hey, comfort zones are overrated anyway. So let's strut our stuff, embrace the unexpected, and show the world just how resilient and extraordinary we can be, my queen!

Now, let's get real for a minute. There were times, my friend, when I felt like adversity had me cornered and I didn't have what it took to face it head-on. I'll admit it, I'd retreat into my shell, hoping the challenges would magically disappear. I'd keep myself busy or hide behind a façade of shyness, wishing that others would leave me alone. It seemed like a convenient escape from opening up and facing my problems head-on. Can you blame me for thinking it might actually work? But you know what? That strategy backfired big time. It only made things worse,

Sassy Lips

prolonging the healing process and creating even more complications down the line.

Lesson learned, my fabulous queen. Avoiding adversity doesn't make it disappear. It just postpones the inevitable and makes it a hell of a lot harder to overcome. So let's ditch the hiding spots, unleash our inner warriors, and face those challenges like the fierce queen we were born to be. Adversity may knock us down, but it sure won't keep us down. We're going to rise, we're going to conquer, and we're going to slay every single obstacle in our path.

You know what's truly awe-inspiring, my queen? As we journey through dark times, something amazing happens within us. We not only become stronger and more resilient, but we also develop this profound understanding and empathy for others fighting their own battles. It's like our shared experiences forge an unbreakable bond, connecting our hearts and souls.

We become beacons of support, offering warm embraces, lending listening ears, and showering hearts with fierce compassion. Adversity opens our eyes to the pain and struggles of others, igniting a burning desire to spread love, kindness, and unwavering support.

Pay close attention, my formidable queen, because I'm about to drop some major truth bombs on you: conquering adversity is like diving into a treasure trove of life-altering lessons that'll leave you slaying like never before. It's no cakewalk, but let me tell you, the wisdom you'll gain along the way is worth its weight in gold. Picture this: as you navigate through trials and tribulations, you'll master the art of resilience, become experts at adapting to every plot twist that life throws your way, and rock the game of problem-solving when faced with those "seriously?" challenges. But here's the best part. Adversity has this badass ability to open your heart to the power of empathy, allowing you to connect on a deeper level with the pain and struggles of others.

But hold up, because we're just getting started. When you fearlessly embrace adversity like the fierce queen you are, get ready for some mind-blowing personal growth. We're talking about a transformation that will have you ruling the world. In the midst of the chaos, I've had an epiphany fit for queens: I'm actually grateful for the wild rollercoaster of adversity that has shaped my life. From the shattered bond between a mother and daughter to the fragments of brokenness scattered like puzzle pieces, every experience has played its part in molding me into the queen I am today. It's through these trials and tribulations that I've truly understood what it means to be broken, to bear the weight of life's challenges. And guess what, my queen? It has ignited a fire within me, a fire that burns with an unyielding desire to guide you on your own journey of self-discovery,

Sassy Lips

to witness you rise above your adversities, and to embrace the extraordinary queen you were destined to be.

Therefore, pay heed, my queen, as this is your moment to radiate. I'm on a mission, and together, we won't back down. I'm here to serve you, my fierce queen, those whose souls have been shattered. I will guide, support, and empower you to tap into your true potential and conquer the world with grace and strength. It's an honor and privilege to walk alongside you on this incredible journey of growth, witnessing your mind-blowing transformation and the impact you'll make in this wild world. My heart beats with an unstoppable desire to ignite your inner spark, to help you unleash your radiant light, and to reign with unapologetic confidence. Let's conquer adversity together, my queen, and show the world the unstoppable force of queens who rise above.

Fearless Queens rise above adversity, turning obstacles into opportunities ~ for ~ growth & empowerment

REIGN LIKE A QUEEN

chapter 4

EMBRACE LIFE WITH SASS & PASSION

Take note, my queen, because I'm about to spill some more sass-infused wisdom on this incredible journey of discovering your passion and owning your purpose in life. Today, I proudly stand as a woman; a queen who has not only found her passion but also struts with unshakable confidence as she fulfils her purpose, despite the challenges she faced from the moment she entered this world.

Let's address the elephant in the room, my fierce queen. Society never fully accepted me right from birth, just because I was born a girl. Can you believe that? But guess what? I refuse to let their narrow-mindedness define me. Instead, I took their rejection and transformed it into fuel for my fire. Life might have thrown some unfair punches my way, but I've learned to embrace my past and use it to fuel my journey towards greatness.

I can almost hear the skeptics saying, "Aroha, are you kidding me? How on earth can you turn that level of trauma into something beautiful?" Well, let me tell you, it wasn't an overnight miracle. It took years of counselling, healing, and surrounding myself with the right people who genuinely had my best interests at heart. I made a conscious decision to seek help, take control of my life, and work towards becoming a better and healthier version of myself. It wasn't easy, but I wasn't about to let my past define my future.

I realized that in order to find the true essence of who I was created to be, I needed to roll up my sleeves and get to work on improving myself in every possible way. You see, greatness doesn't just drop out of the sky, my queen. If you want to succeed and fulfil your purpose in life, you've got to be willing to put in the hard yards. Want a body that makes heads turn? Lace up those sneakers and hit the gym. Craving knowledge and personal growth? Invest in education

Sassy Lips

and feed your hungry mind. And if you're longing for a better mindset that propels you forward, seek guidance from the right professionals who can help you unleash your greatest potential.

It's time to ditch the lazy excuses and step up your game, my fierce queen. Nothing great ever comes easy, and it's only the diligent ones who are willing to put in the effort and commitment that see real results. So, let's lace up our combat boots and embark on a thrilling journey of discovering our passion and purpose in life.

But let me tell you, this journey is not just about stumbling upon a passing interest or a fleeting hobby. Oh no, it's about delving deep into the very core of who you are. It's about unearthing those hidden desires and aligning your actions with your authentic self. Get ready for a wild ride filled with experiences that will challenge you, push you out of your comfort zone, and test your tenacity.

In the midst of this exploration, grant yourself the freedom to embrace the unknown and open yourself to new possibilities. We're not about playing it safe, my queen. It's time to step outside the boundaries of what we've known and venture into uncharted territories. This is where the magic happens — where we discover hidden passions and talents we never even knew existed. It's time to break free from that confining box and get relaxed about being fabulously uncomfortable.

But let me share something deeply personal with you, my fierce queen. The truth is, everything within you will naturally resist change. Your mind will try to keep you confined within the safety of your comfort zone, where familiarity reigns supreme. Your emotions might throw a tantrum, and even your instincts will scream for you to stay put. But I'm here to tell you, my queen, that growth, fulfilment, and true happiness lie beyond those boundaries.

Yes, the journey ahead will have its fair share of bumps and hurdles. It will push you to your limits, demand unwavering commitment, and force you to face your deepest fears head-on. But mark my words, my fierce queen, it's all part of the process. It's through these challenges that we grow, evolve, and become the unstoppable queen we were born to be.

So, when doubt tries to rain on your parade, remember to trust yourself and the incredible journey you're on. Embrace the discomfort, the uncertainty, and the moments of vulnerability. Believe in the limitless strength, resilience, and untapped potential that reside within you, just waiting to be unleashed. You're capable of defying all odds and shining your light brighter than ever before.

Sassy Lips

I won't sugarcoat it, my queen. The road ahead won't be a smooth ride, but let me assure you, it'll be worth every single drop of sweat and tears. Take that leap of faith, embrace the challenges and uncertainties with a fierce smile on your face. Trust in your own abilities and the infinite possibilities that lie ahead. Believe in yourself and get ready to embark on a life-altering journey of passion, purpose, and unapologetic transformation. It's time to live life on your own terms and unleash your reign as the unstoppable queen you were always meant to be! It's time to embrace life with sass and passion, and rule with confidence, grace and authority!

Now let's dive into these questions with some serious sass and confidence. Get ready to unleash your inner queen and gain those valuable insights into your passions and purpose.

First up, we're talking activities and hobbies that set your heart on fire. I'm talking about the ones that make you feel alive, bring you immense joy, and leave you feeling fulfilled. Get ready to embrace the things that make you say, "Finally! This is what life is all about!"

Now, tell me, my queen, when do you feel like a ball of pure energy? When does your whole being light up with enthusiasm and total engagement? We're seeking those moments where you're so captivated by what you're doing that time seems to slip away.

Hold on tight, because these are the moments that will guide you towards your passions.

Let's stoke the flames of your fire, my fierce queen. What topics or issues set your soul ablaze? What sparks that intense desire to make a positive change in the world? We're tapping into that fire within you — the one that drives you to create a massive impact. Get ready to ignite change like the amazing queen you are!

You've got natural talents and strengths, my queen. These are your secret weapons that will propel you towards your passions. Embrace them and leverage them like the fierce force of nature you are. It's time to unleash your powers and pursue what comes naturally to you.

Now, let's talk about getting lost in the moment. You know what I mean. Those activities or pursuits that make time vanish because you're so absorbed in them. We're diving deep into these immersive experiences because they hold the key to your passions. Get ready to lose track of time like the boss queen you are!

Remember those dreams and aspirations you held dear as a wide-eyed child? Well, my queen, it's time to bring them back to life! Dust them off, breathe life into them, and set them free. The time has come to

Sassy Lips

chase those dreams and make them a reality. Let your inner child run wild!

You've got values and principles that guide your life, my queen. These are the rock-solid foundations that will shape your passions. Align your desires with these guiding stars and watch how your passions become a force to be reckoned with. Stay true to yourself, my fierce queen.

In your free time, where does your heart naturally gravitate? What activities call out to you when the world is your oyster? Embrace these natural inclinations because they hold the seeds of your passions. It's time to let your instincts guide you towards greatness.

You're a queen on a mission. What impact do you want to leave on this crazy world? How can your passions contribute to that grand vision? It's time to unleash your passion and let it become the driving force behind the impact you were born to make. Get ready to rock the world!

Enough with the waiting game, my sassy queen. It's time to take action! What steps can you take right now, in this very moment, to explore and nurture your passions? Even if it's on a small scale, every step counts. Grab life by the horns and unleash your passion, one bold move at a time!

So, my fierce queen, reflect on these questions, dive into your answers, and embrace the journey of self-discovery with sass and confidence. Be open to new experiences, embrace growth, and follow those sparks that set your soul ablaze. Get ready to live a life fueled by passion and purpose. You've got this, my queen!

A *Fearless Queen*
knows that her power lies
~ in ~
embracing her unique journey,
owning her story
and *paving* her own path.

FEARLESS QUEENS

PART TWO

EQUIPPING *my* QUEENS

EQUIP AND CONQUER

Sassy Lips

EMPOWERING FIERCE QUEENS WITH THE RIGHT TOOLS & RESOURCES

My queen, it took me a while to find what truly set my soul ablaze. I was hopping from one passion to another like a fierce diva caught in the "shiny syndrome." One minute, I was belting it out as a full-time vocalist, and the next, I was daydreaming about ruling the entertainment industry or guiding others as a mentor. Little did I know, those shifts were all part of the fabulous journey that led me exactly where I was meant to be: a formidable business and life coach.

Trial and error, my dear, played a major role in my quest for passion. I danced through different paths, gaining precious insights and discovering what truly clicked with my heart. Each experience, even if it didn't lead me straight to my ultimate calling, gifted me valuable lessons and molded my understanding of what I craved deep down.

Once I finally found my true passion, I realized I was missing a few tools in my fabulous arsenal. I had the fire within, the dreams, and the ambition, but I lacked the necessary knowledge and resources to make my mark. Shifting from being a mere employee to running my own empire took me way out of my comfort zone. I quickly learned that running a business required a whole different set of skills than just punching a clock for someone else.

At first, I relied on my previous work ethic and what I thought I knew, thinking I could simply "wing it" and slay like a queen. But let me tell you, darling, that "fake it till you make it" mantra only gets you so far before reality slaps you in the face with obstacles and challenges that demand a more solid foundation.

I had an epiphany, my fabulous queen. In order to truly thrive and unleash my passion like a fierce force of nature, I had to equip myself with the right tools and resources. I went on a mission to seek wisdom and guidance from industry experts who knew their stuff. I knew I had to invest in my own growth and development, both on a personal and professional level. So, I embarked on a journey of continuous learning, attending mind-blowing workshops, and seeking the mentorship of those who had walked the path of success before me. I was building an unbreakable foundation to support my dazzling journey. Because let's be real: passion alone won't cut it. You need the knowledge, the strategies, and the know-how to conquer the world just like the empowered queen you are.

But there is more to tell you. Oh, honey, on my journey from misguided confidence to a fierce dose of reality, from arrogance to awesomeness, my mentors schooled me in the art of embracing humility while on the road to entrepreneurship. With over two decades of experience in management, finance, marketing, and business, I strutted around thinking I had it all figured out. I believed my massive knowledge and expertise automatically made me a queen at any entrepreneurial endeavor. Oh, how wrong I was, darling!

Picture this, my queen: I found myself engaging in highly charged debates with my mentors. I defended my ideas and methods with all my sass, convinced they were superior to anything those mentors could offer. I boldly proclaimed, "That's not how you create a business! I've been in this game for years, and your approaches simply don't align with mine."

But let me tell you, beneath that stubborn façade, there was a hint of arrogance instead of a genuine willingness to learn and grow. Ouch!

But hold up! Even in my defiance, I couldn't ignore the truth that slapped me right in the face. Deep down, I knew my mentors' success spoke volumes; they were true entrepreneurs in every sense. They had satisfied clients and bank accounts that were flourishing like a glorious garden. And what struck me most was their genuine love for what they do — serving others with passion. Despite my resistance, I couldn't deny that their ideas and strategies had some serious merit.

My mentors didn't give me the boot or dismiss my misguided confidence like yesterday's fashion. They saw beyond my initial arrogance and recognized the potential hidden beneath my sassy exterior. They understood that I was just a rookie on my entrepreneurial journey, and they had the wisdom, tools, and resources to help me build my dream empire. Instead of waving me goodbye, they extended grace and patience, offering their guidance and expertise to shape my fierce entrepreneurial mindset.

I am forever grateful for their unwavering support. They saw my hunger for growth and development, and they fanned that spark within me until it turned into an unstoppable flame. They understood the unique challenges of entrepreneurship and the importance of equipping me with the right skills, knowledge, and mindset to slay in the business world.

But hold onto your fabulous hats, because their mentorship went way beyond just sharing their wisdom and experience. They became my international extended family, my fierce circle of support. They opened the doors to invaluable resources and connected me with a network of like-minded individuals who inspired and collaborated with me. They pushed me to attend mind-blowing workshops, seminars, and industry events where I could expand my knowledge and rub shoulders with other passionate entrepreneurs.

Looking back, I now realize the invaluable role my mentors played in shaping my fabulous journey. Their guidance and belief in my potential helped me navigate the complexities of entrepreneurship. Their wisdom and support gave me the confidence to embrace new ideas, take calculated risks, and conquer challenges like a true queen. They taught me the art of humility, curiosity, and a genuine willingness to learn.

So, if you find yourself on a similar adventure, my sassy queen, remember that humility and an open mind are your secret weapons. Surround yourself with mentors who have danced the dance of entrepreneurship, and be ready to soak in their fierce guidance. Embrace every opportunity to expand your knowledge, attend industry events, and connect with fellow go-getters. Success is never achieved alone, my queen. It's a wild ride of collaboration, continuous learning, and the boldness to adapt.

Now, my fabulous queen, armed with the lessons I've learned, I approach every new endeavor with an open heart and an open mind. I know that the journey of entrepreneurship is a never-ending dance with endless things to learn and discover. I am forever grateful for the mentors who believed in me, challenged me, and armed me with the tools and resources to thrive. Their impact and support throughout my journey are something I'll always treasure.

But wait, there's more! I've come to realize that true fulfilment comes not just from achieving our own goals but also from helping others soar to new heights. It's a beautiful cycle of growth and support. So, I've made it my mission to pay it forward by becoming a mentor, coach, and guide to those who are chasing their own passions and dreams, especially in the fierce world of business. It's a beautiful opportunity and blessing when you get to do what you love, and you love what you do.

So, if you're feeling lost or unsure, remember this: you don't have to strut alone. I'm here to extend a fabulous helping hand, to share my own experiences, and to cheer you on every step of the way. Together, we'll explore your passions, identify your strengths, and

Sassy Lips

chart a course towards a future that's both fulfilling and wildly successful. Trust me, I understand the challenges and uncertainties that come with pursuing a passion or starting a business, and I'm here to provide fierce support and encouragement to my queens.

No matter where you find yourself in your journey, my queen, always remember this: You possess the power within you to create the life you desire. And with guidance, support, and a truckload of sass, along with being equipped with the right tools and resources to fulfil your greatest potential, you'll be amazed at what you can achieve. So, let's get started, shall we? It's time to slay and stay focused on your fabulous dreams!

A *Fearless Queen,* equipped and empowered, *reigns* with *unshakable authority.*

FROM VISION TO REALITY

chapter 6

Sassy Lips

BUILDING UNSTOPPABLE EMPIRES WITH A QUEEN'S FOUNDATION

As I chased my business dreams back in the day, it was a thrilling time, filled with hope and a sprinkle of uncertainty — actually, scratch that — there's a whole lot of uncertainty. Picture this: I had my goals set, and I gathered all the knowledge, tools, and resources fit for a queen. But something was missing — something that would slay from the very beginning. And that's when my amazing niece swooped in to save the day!

She was running her own fabulous clothing and home decor empire. And guess what? She knew just the queen who could help me — her incredible business coach, a true game-changer! With excitement dripping from her voice, she told me, "Aunty, you absolutely have to meet my business coach." Now, you know that, when a queen like her recommends something — you listen. Inspired by my niece's success, I couldn't resist this golden opportunity, even though I was feeling a mix of nerves and excitement. Because actions, darling, speak louder than words, and seeing my niece slay the game made me hungry for the secrets this coach had up her perfectly tailored sleeve.

But let me give you a little friendly advice, my queen: when you're searching for the right mentor or coach, do your homework, because we don't swim with sharks, we ride the waves like queens. There are plenty of options out there, so make sure you find someone who matches your values and has a proven track record of success. Trust me, it's worth putting in that extra effort, because queens like us deserve nothing but the best.

With the meeting set, I decided to bring my daughter along for some extra support and to make sure not a single drop of wisdom escaped our fabulous minds. Little did I know that this encounter would completely change my life!

Sassy Lips

As I spilled my dreams and aspirations to this potential coach, she unfolded a step-by-step process to build an empire fit for a queen. It was beyond amazing! Every piece of advice she gave felt like a perfectly fitting puzzle piece in my grand vision. These ideas and strategies were no empty theories, honey — they were battle-tested methods that could turn my dreams into a reality that slays. I couldn't help but get emotional — tears of joy welled up in my eyes. It felt like I was witnessing a truly extraordinary transformation right before me!

I must admit, there were moments when I questioned my worth and wondered if I deserved all this success. But this incredible coach saw right through my doubts. She listened — I mean, really listened — and addressed all my concerns and worries with grace and understanding. It was a connection so deep and profound that it filled my heart with renewed confidence and excitement. And let me tell you, darling, I knew this was the real deal!

As my daughter and I travelled back home, we couldn't contain our excitement. We talked for hours about the incredible opportunities and possibilities that lay before us. Finally, I had found what I had been searching for — a clear roadmap to build a solid business foundation that actually works! The car was buzzing with anticipation as we envisioned the fabulous journey that awaited us. But there was one thing left — I needed to spill the tea with my husband. Would he be providing support or would he raise concerns? The time had come to find out.

I couldn't wait to spill all the details to my husband, but as expected, he had questions — oh, so many questions! And that's when our power couple dynamic truly shone. You see, when it comes to making decisions for our family, we are an unstoppable team. We bring together our unique expertise and perspectives to find the absolute best path forward.

My husband, by nature, is the ultimate observer. He doesn't jump into things without thoughtful consideration. He takes the time to investigate, analyze, and weigh the pros and cons. He's a man of wisdom, guided by logic instead of emotions. And then there's me, the adventurous queen, always ready to break the rules and think outside the box. I thrive on challenges and, well, I might have a bit of impatience when fabulous opportunities arise. But guess what, my queen? We balance each other perfectly.

Together, we dived into deep discussions and royal deliberations about the next step in our journey. We didn't just consider the impact on our business but also on our fabulous family. It was crucial to us that we made the right decision, one that would benefit everyone involved. After thoughtful conversations and regal contemplation, we both agreed: investing in a business coach was the way to go. And let me spill the tea, darling; it turned out to be the best investment this queen has ever made.

That decision opened doors to a whole new kingdom of possibilities. The guidance and support I received from my business coach were simply priceless. With her expertise, I gained clarity, direction, and all the tools I needed to conquer the entrepreneurial landscape.

It was like having a trusted ally by my side — someone who believed in my dreams and helped me turn them into regal reality. With a solid foundation in place, I felt ready to embark on an epic journey towards my future. Little did I know that this was just the beginning of an awe-inspiring adventure that awaited me.

But here's the real deal: I knew that this journey would require some serious commitments from me. It meant showing up on time, being open to new ideas, doing my homework, and respecting not only my coach's time but also my own. Integrity was everything, and I made a promise to myself to dive into this wholeheartedly, like the true queen I am.

Now, let's talk about the financial investment, darling. Let me spill the tea — it was no small change. But guess what? I knew deep down that what we invested would be worth every dollar and then some. I understood that it wasn't just about the money; it was about the amazing benefits and the impact it would have on my future and the future of my queendom.

It's what I like to call the ripple effect, where the outcome of the investment goes far beyond just myself. This realization came to me on my journey as an entrepreneur, where I began to appreciate the true worth of investing in myself, my dreams, and securing a fabulous future for my family. Building a solid foundation for my queendom was worth every dollar invested, darling.

So, my fellow queen, let me empower you. Embrace the understanding that building a solid business foundation is essential, and investing in yourself is a fierce decision. See it as an opportunity to grow, learn, and transform your life into the reign of a queen. Instead of getting caught up solely in the costs, shift your mindset to envision the incredible benefits that await you. Remember, the path of an entrepreneur is an ongoing journey of growth and self-discovery. Every step you take and every investment you make is a testament to your belief in your own queendom, a brighter future, and the fulfilment of your dreams.
You are building your unstoppable empires with a Queen's foundation.
Now, go out there and rule the world, my fabulous queen!

A *Fearless Queen*
builds an empire that
defies limits
~ and ~
inspires the world.

SLAY QUEEN SUPREME

chapter 7

CONQUER AND SEIZE EVERY FABULOUS OPPORTUNITY

Get ready to sashay back to 2018, my fabulous queen, a time filled with excitement and unexpected surprises that had me living my best life. I was working my business game like a boss, thanks to my amazing business coach, who had been guiding me on my entrepreneurial journey. But hold onto your crowns, because an incredible opportunity was about to knock on my door, catching not just me but my entire family off guard!

Picture this, my queen: it was the holiday season, and we were getting ready to slay Christmas and ring in the new year with open arms. And as if that wasn't enough, my youngest son's 21st birthday was just around the corner in February, adding an extra sprinkle of joy to our plans. Life was bursting with anticipation and those special moments that make memories shine.

But one day, while I was doing my boss babe thing, my phone started ringing like crazy. It was my business coach on the line, bursting with excitement. She couldn't wait to spill the tea about her mind-blowing news. She was heading to the USA to rub shoulders with other fabulous entrepreneurs and attend an event called Funnel Hacking Live, hosted by none other than the multi-millionaire CEO and co-founder of ClickFunnels, Russell Brunson. Now, at that time, I had no clue who this Russell Brunson was, so naturally, I asked my coach to give me the 411. And, darlings, let me tell you, she went on and on about how ClickFunnels had become a major powerhouse in the marketing software world. I was left absolutely shaken by their epic success.

But the conversation didn't stop there, my queen. Oh no, my coach was about to drop a bombshell that would leave me gagging. She spilled the tea that she was embarking on a nine-week business trip across 8 states in America, collaborating, networking, and

Sassy Lips

learning from the crème de la crème of the industry. And guess what? Here's where it gets truly fabulous: She extended an invitation for me to partake in the nine-week business venture, which encompassed a cruise to the enchanting Bahamas. During this time, I would seize the opportunity to connect with Russell and other remarkable entrepreneurs, all while expanding my business knowledge.Can you believe it, queens? It was like a dream come true, but with a fierce time limit. She gave me just 24 hours to decide because we'd be flying out the day after New Year!

Naturally, my jaw dropped to the floor, and my husband, sensing the commotion, couldn't help but ask, "What's going on, honey?" So, I spilled all the juicy details of my conversation with my coach. In my mind, I was already expecting my husband to shut down the whole idea.

I mean, leaving our family behind for nine weeks in a foreign land, surrounded by strangers? That was a definite no-go, or so I thought. But hold onto your tiara, my queen, because my husband's response completely blew me away. He looked me straight in the eyes and said, "Honey, this is the opportunity you've been waiting for to take your business to the next level. You should totally go for it! Opportunities like this are as rare, and we can't let them slip through our fingers." Can you believe it? I was in a state of utter shock, overwhelmed by my husband's unwavering support.

With the whole family gathered around, we had a heart-to-heart, spilling all the tea about this incredible opportunity that had unexpectedly come my way. And let me tell you, the love and enthusiasm that radiated from each of my children were absolutely off the charts. Without a moment's hesitation, they chimed in, their voices bursting with excitement and encouragement. "Mum, you have to seize this opportunity! It's absolutely amazing, and we couldn't be happier for you. This adventure will be a game-changer, and you'll gain invaluable knowledge from those incredible entrepreneurs. We'll miss you, of course, but this is a once-in-a-lifetime opportunity, Mum. We love you to the moon and back, and we wholeheartedly believe you should go for it!"

Their words wrapped around me like a warm hug, filling my heart with love and reassurance. It was an outpouring of support and a reminder of just how blessed I was to have such an extraordinary family. Their unwavering belief in me and their genuine excitement for the journey ahead made the decision that much easier. With their blessings and love in my heart, I knew I was ready to embark on this extraordinary adventure, knowing that my family had my back every step of the way.

After thoughtful consideration and many heart-to-heart conversations, we made the decision together — yours truly was going on this incredible adventure,

Sassy Lips

even if it meant traveling with people I had only recently met. The opportunity was just too fabulous to pass up, my queen!

With our plans set in motion, we devoted ourselves to creating the most memorable Christmas for our family. We sat down and plotted how we would celebrate my son's 21st birthday in a special way, even in my absence. I have to admit, the thought of missing one of my children's birthdays tugged at my heartstrings.

But my son, being the absolute star he is, reassured me with the most loving words. He said, "Mum, we are one hundred percent behind you. This experience will benefit all of us in the long run. Go and seize this opportunity like the fierce queen you are. We'll have an incredible celebration waiting for you when you return." In that moment, surrounded by love and encouragement from my husband and children, I felt an overwhelming sense of gratitude. I felt blessed beyond measure to have such an incredible, loving, and supportive family.

So, my queen, fasten your crowns and get ready for the ride of a lifetime. This adventure was about to change everything, and I couldn't wait to see what the future held. Life was about to get even more fabulous, and I was ready to slay every step of the way!

Let me take you back to the year 2018, my queen, when I found myself on a wild adventure to America, a place I never thought I'd visit. But hey, I've learned never to say never, especially when it comes to embracing the unexpected. New York, Miami, Los Angeles, Nashville, New Orleans, Las Vegas, Sunny Isles, Florida, and the Bahamas became my playground for entrepreneurship. Little did I know that not everyone in my extended family would be on board with my fabulous plans. Oh, the audacity!

Let me spill the tea about a part of my journey that involved facing opposition, not just from strangers, but from those closest to me. Oh, honey, pursuing greatness often comes with resistance, and let me tell you, I faced it head-on. Insecurities and fears were thrown at me left and right, coming from my family and loved ones. Some even claimed they received divine messages telling me not to go. Can you believe the nerve? But in moments like these, my queen, we must pause and reflect. It was time for me to shed the expectations of others and step outside my comfort zone, ready to slay.

But fear not, for every fierce queen needs a circle of amazing friends to confide in. And let me tell you, I was blessed with some long-time friends who knew me inside out and could serve up clarity and support like no other. They reassured me that the comments and opposition I faced were rooted in their own insecurities and not in any genuine concern for my well-being. Can you believe the audacity of their insecurities in trying to bring me down? Absolutely not, darling!

With their encouragement and guidance, I became even more determined to embrace this opportunity for growth with open arms. Oh, there were nerves and emotions about leaving my husband and family for nine weeks, but deep down, I knew it was a crucial step for my personal and professional development. It was time for me, Aroha, to soar to new heights, expand my fabulous mindset, learn from the best, and establish a legacy that will create a ripple effect of inspiration for generations to follow. Oh yes, serving those incredible individuals I was destined to meet and supporting them in achieving their own entrepreneurial dreams? Darling, it was a dream come true!

By embracing this fierce journey, despite the mixed reactions I received, I showed the world my determination and resilience. It was a powerful reminder that I am the queen of my own path, even when faced with opposition. And let me tell you, I am eternally grateful for the support of my true friends, their prayers, and the inner conviction that led me to seize this opportunity for growth and transformation.

Now, my fabulous queen, I want to leave you with this: seizing opportunities feels like opening a door to unexplored territories, where every step is infused with excitement and where possibilities are endless, and potential knows no bounds. It's like opening a door to a world where dreams become reality and extraordinary experiences await. When we wholeheartedly embrace and act upon the opportunities that come our way, we unlock a treasure trove of amazing benefits that enrich our lives beyond imagination.

Seizing opportunities isn't just about personal and professional growth, my queen — it's about nurturing a lifelong love affair with learning and exploration. Each opportunity becomes a glittering gem on our educational journey, allowing us to acquire new knowledge, refine our skills, and stay at the forefront of our chosen fields. We attend workshops, conferences, and dive headfirst into further education, driven by our unstoppable curiosity and passion for continuous growth.

But it doesn't stop there, my queen. Seizing opportunities also connects us with kindred spirits and broadens our horizons. As we venture into uncharted territory, we encounter remarkable individuals who share our passions and aspirations. These connections often blossom into collaborations, mentorships, and lifelong friendships that provide unwavering support, guidance, and inspiration. Can you imagine the power of that, my queen? It's like finding a squad of fabulous individuals who uplift us every step of the way.

Sassy Lips

Above all, seizing opportunities brings us closer to a life filled with purpose and fulfilment. It's about mustering the courage to pursue our dreams and goals, smashing through barriers that dare to hold us back. We embark on a path that aligns with our deepest desires, creating a life that brings us genuine joy and satisfaction. It's an awe-inspiring adventure that allows us to express ourselves fully and unleash our fabulousness upon the world.

So, my queen, keep those eyes wide open, for you are equipped to seize the opportunities that twirl their way into your life. Grab hold of those precious moments, for they hold the key to a world of wonders, personal growth, and unforgettable experiences. The journey may not always be easy but, trust me, the rewards are beyond measure. So go forth, my queen, and seize those opportunities like the fierce, unstoppable forces of nature you are!

A *Fearless Queen*

conquers challenges
~ and ~
fearlessly seizes

every opportunity that comes her way.

PART THREE

EVOVLE,
my
QUEENS

GET READY TO EMBRACE CHANGE

Sassy Lips

EMBRACE CHANGE LIKE SASSY LIPS & FEARLESS QUEENS

My queen, let me spill the tea about my past worries! When anything new or different came my way, I used to get all worked up. It didn't matter if it was a major change or something as tiny as starting a new gig, meeting new people, or jetting off to a new place. I'd get overwhelmed, and fear would swoop in before I even gave it a chance. Can you believe it? It even robbed me of precious beauty sleep. Can you relate, my queen?

But guess what? As time went on, I had a major awakening. All that fretting I was doing? It didn't change a thing. It just drained my fabulous energy. So I decided to switch things up. Instead of assuming the worst, I started opening my mind to new, fabulous experiences. And guess what, darling? I began to see that worrying was holding me back from all the excitement and possibilities that come with change. Can you imagine missing out on all that fabulousness?

I even had a little heart-to-heart with myself. "Hey, Aroha," I said, "Why are you getting so wrapped up in things you can't control? What's the point of stressing over tomorrow when today is right here, just waiting for you to slay it? This could be a freaking incredible opportunity!"

So, as I continued on my journey as an entrepreneur, I made the choice to embrace change and uncertainty like a queen boss. Life has its ups and downs, and I realized that making the most of every situation is what it's all about.

Letting go of unnecessary worries and seeing each change as a chance to grow has made such a huge difference in my fabulous life. I can't even express how much I appreciate the freedom that comes with it. It's like a weight that has been snatched off my shoulders!

Sassy Lips

But you know what? The best part is that I've come to love change. Oh yes, honey, you heard me right. I am all about it now, especially when it brings challenges. Those situations that push me out of my comfort zone? They're like magical doors opening to new possibilities. Sure, learning to be comfortable with being uncomfortable wasn't a piece of cake, but let me tell you, it was so worth it.

My queen, I was about to embark on one of the most monumental changes in my life. I'm jetting off to a foreign country, leaving my fabulous family behind, traveling all over America with fierce people I just met, meeting incredible entrepreneurs who are a little intimidating, making new fabulous friends, and expanding my knowledge into uncharted territory. It's going to take me so far out of my comfort zone that it's not even funny. But you know what, my queen? I thought to myself, I am so ready for this. I'm ready to embrace this change with open arms because, deep down, I know it's going to be a transformative experience that will have me slaying like never before.

The winds of change are blowing, and I'm sailing right into them, ready to conquer whatever comes my way. So, bring it on! Little did I know I was about to hop on the most exhilarating emotional rollercoaster ride ever.

Through my own transformative journey, I gained self-confidence, belief, and a fierce sense of purpose. Now, I'm here to teach my fabulous clients how to embrace change and discover their own worth. But let me tell you, when I meet my fierce queen, I give them a heads up before we dive into coaching together. Here's how the conversation goes: "If you choose me as your coach and decide to join my coaching program, get ready for a major shakeup in your world. I mean, almost everything in your life will be challenged — mentally, physically, emotionally, and even financially." Exciting, right? Well, here's the deal, honey: we're about to slay some serious change, and let me tell you, it can get pretty uncomfortable. We're going to turn every stone to make sure we uncover anything that's not serving you. But don't you fret, because on the other side of this fabulous transformation, you're going to discover your true worth as a person and as a queen boss. So, are you ready to buckle up for this wild ride? Their initial reaction is always one of excitement mixed with a dash of apprehension, but deep down, they are ready to embrace it. They know they're in a safe space to shine.

Now, let's talk about embracing change, my queen. It's not just about dealing with external transformations; it's also an opportunity to explore a whole rollercoaster of emotions that usually tag along. When we embark on this fabulous journey, we open ourselves up to a wide range of feelings, from pure exhilaration to a touch of uncertainty.

Sassy Lips

One of the emotional challenges we might encounter is the fear of the unknown. Change messes with our fabulous routines and leaves us wondering what the future holds. It's totally natural to feel a bit nervous and question if we're making the right decisions or if we've got what it takes to conquer this new path. Sometimes, these emotions can even lead to a little self-doubt, making us question our abilities and whether we're ready to handle all the changes that are coming our way.

Another challenge we face is the resistance to letting go of the past. We often cling to what's familiar, even when it's no longer serving our fabulous selves. But guess what? Change invites us to release our grip on old ways of being and embrace fresh possibilities. Now, bidding farewell to those comfy habits, relationships, or beliefs can be tough, and it's absolutely okay to feel a little nostalgic or experience a sense of grief during this process. Let those fierce emotions flow, my queen.

And you know what else changes bring up? Vulnerability. Stepping into new territory means taking risks and opening ourselves up to the possibility of failure, rejection, or judgment. It's only natural that this vulnerability might make us feel a bit uneasy. After all, we're putting ourselves out there, and there's always a chance of not meeting expectations or facing criticism. But guess what?

Embracing vulnerability takes some serious courage, and it often leads to incredible growth opportunities. We're queens, and we're not afraid to slay, right?

So, as we strut our way through this journey, it's crucial to acknowledge and honour these emotional challenges that pop up along the way. Give yourself permission to feel the full spectrum of emotions that arise during times of change. It's completely normal to experience a mix of excitement, fear, resistance, and vulnerability. Take the time and space you need to sit with these emotions, allowing them to be heard and understood.

Just a fab reminder, though: while emotions play a major role, it's equally important to gather all the information, seek advice from trusted sources, follow your fabulous intuition, and find that inner peace before making any major decisions. It's all about finding the perfect balance between your fierce heart and your brilliant mind.

During this glamorous process, make sure you surround yourself with a support system that uplifts and encourages you. Seek solace in your fabulous friends, family, or mentors who understand what you're going through. But, darling, be wise in your choice of confidantes. Share your thoughts and emotions with people you trust.

So, my fabulous queen, I'm throwing this question

Sassy Lips

at you: Are you ready to conquer this incredible journey of change and make it your own? Trust me, the adventure ahead is absolutely worth it. We're about to slay like never before! Let"s do this and show the world who the true queens are!

As a *Queen,*
~I~
embrace change
with open arms, for it is through
transformation
that I reign supreme and unlock
infinite possibilities.

QUEEN'S GUIDE

chapter 9

Sassy Lips

UNLEASHING LASTING TRANSFORMATION *Like a Queen!*

My fabulous queen! We often stumble upon mind-blowing stories of transformation from people with diverse backgrounds, cultures, and seriously challenging experiences. Today, let me spill the tea about a heartfelt conversation I recently had with someone very close to me, whom I will refer to as Queen Mama.

This amazing queen of mine just entered the loving embrace of our Lord Jesus, but not before dropping some major truth bombs. Allow me to spill the details:

Queen Mama: "I'm not ready to leave this world, darling. There's still so much I want to accomplish, but not enough time. I don't feel like I've done enough. I'm not ready to go, but hey, I know my timing is in the Lord's hands."

Me: "Hold up, Queen Mama, because I've got something to share that I also shared with a family member before she departed this realm. Not all of us are meant to be in the spotlight, dazzling on a public platform for all to see. Some of us make a significant impact through our hidden work behind closed doors, those intimate one-on-one interactions, and those everyday conversations that leave a lasting mark. Words of encouragement, supporting families, giving financial aid, offering comfort, and spreading truths with love can have a mind-blowing effect, just as powerful as those who shine on grand stages. Have you ever realized the tremendous impact you've had on people's lives throughout the years? Just look at that constant stream of visitors, calls, and messages you receive, Queen Mama!

We may not always witness the full extent of our influence, but let me tell you, those seeds of goodness you've planted in their lives will sprout and grow for generations to come. That's what I call

Sassy Lips

lasting transformation; its impact spreads across time and is shared from one generation to another. And if you ever do get a glimpse of the direct effect, consider it a true blessing.

In a nutshell, that heartfelt conversation with Queen Mama reminded me that our impact goes beyond the glitz and glam of public recognition. Oh no, no, no! It's those transformative moments you may not always witness, but let me assure you, the everyday acts of kindness, support, and love we offer can have a profound and lasting effect, even if we don't always see the full extent of them. That, my queen, is the secret to lasting transformation. So, let's keep sowing those seeds of goodness and trust that they will bear fruit for generations to come, personally and in business.

Listen closely, my fabulous queen, because this conversation has lit a fire within me, and I'm here to reach out to all those fierce divas who have ever felt unworthy, doubted themselves, but still held onto that dream of success. It's time to gather 'round, my queens, because I've got a message for each and every one of you.

You may have faced moments when the world tried to dim your sparkle, when the doubters and haters made you question your worth. But guess what, my queen? You are worthy, oh so worthy, and your dreams deserve to be unleashed with a vengeance!

FEARLESS QUEENS

I see you, my queen, with that fire burning in your souls — a dream that refuses to be extinguished. It's time to shake off those doubts, cast aside the negativity, and step into your power. You have what it takes, and it's time to show the world just how powerful and unstoppable you truly are.

So, my queen, gather your courage, harness that self-belief, and let's slay the game together. We're here to support each other, to lift each other up, and to prove all those naysayers wrong. This is your time to shine, to seize your dreams, and to make them a reality that's so fierce it'll leave everyone gasping for breath.

No more playing small, my queen. It's time to rise and claim your rightful place on the throne of success. Believe in yourself, embrace your worthiness, and let your dreams soar higher than the highest stiletto. The world is waiting for your brilliance, and I know, without a shadow of a doubt, that you will succeed beyond your wildest imagination.

So, my queen, let's unleash that inner power, that unwavering determination, and let the world know that you are here to conquer and reign supreme. Believe in yourself, embrace your dreams, and let's make this journey one for the history books.

Together, we will rise, we will succeed, and we will leave a legacy that future queens will look up to. It's time to take the stage, my queen, and let your radiance illuminate the world. Are you ready to slay? Let's do this!

Now, let's shift gears and dive deep into the world of the solo entrepreneur, where we're about to create a lasting transformation in your business. Can you picture it, my fierce queen? You, as a solo entrepreneur, are standing at the edge of starting your own business, ready to slay the game. Buckle up, because we're about to unveil the secrets that will guide you on this journey of lasting transformation:

Listen closely, my fabulous queen, because I'm about to invite you on a journey that will take your dreams and transform them into a booming business! You have the power, my darling, to turn your wildest visions into a reality that'll leave everyone gagging in awe. But let me spill some reality: it's going to take some serious hard work and unwavering commitment. Don't fret, my queen, because you won't be alone on this journey. We're in this together, supporting and uplifting one another every step of the way. With a fierce passion burning in your hearts, an unstoppable adaptability to conquer any challenge, and an unwavering commitment to growth, we're about to create something truly remarkable. So, my queen, are you ready to grab hold of your dreams, sprinkle them with your unique essence, and turn them into a thriving business empire? Get ready to slay like never before, and let's make this dream-to-business transformation a reality!

First and foremost, let's talk about your vision. Take a moment to channel your inner diva and reflect on why you started this journey in the first place. Connect with your deep-rooted purpose and envision the incredible impact you want to make with your business. This vision will be your guiding light, propelling you forward even in the face of the toughest challenges.

As a solo entrepreneur, adaptability is your superpower, darling. Embrace change with open arms and a flexible mindset. Be willing to adjust your plans and strategies as you learn and grow. Stay curious, explore emerging trends, and remain open to new opportunities that may strut their way into your path.

By staying adaptable, you'll be able to slay obstacles and seize exciting possibilities. And remember, always be willing to learn and walk with grace and humility toward your fabulous success.

My queen, as a solo entrepreneur, you are the heart and soul of your business. It's time to empower yourself! Cultivate fierce self-belief and confidence in your abilities. Surround yourself with a supportive network of mentors, friends, or fellow entrepreneurs who can offer guidance, encouragement, and some well-deserved snaps. Seek out resources and educational opportunities to enhance your skills. By investing in yourself, you'll unlock your true potential and achieve remarkable results. Remember, you're the queen of your kingdom!

Customer-centricity is key for a solo entrepreneur, darling. Take the time to truly understand your target audience — their needs, desires, and pain points. Build genuine connections with your customers and listen to their feedback. Strive to create exceptional experiences that address their specific challenges. By putting your customers at the center of everything you do, you'll cultivate loyal relationships that fuel the growth of your fabulous business. Keep them coming back for more, my queen!

As a solo entrepreneur, you wear multiple crowns, but never forget to be a friendly leader to yourself. Celebrate every small victory, my fabulous queen, and show yourself compassion during setbacks. Embrace a growth mindset and view failures as valuable learning opportunities. Seek out collaboration and support from like-minded individuals in your industry. Surround yourself with positivity and seek out mentorship or join entrepreneurial communities where you can learn, share insights, and receive encouragement. And above all, my queen, never give up on your dreams! You're destined for greatness.

Your journey as a solo entrepreneur is a continuous process of improvement and learning. Embrace your curiosity, my curious queen, and explore new ideas and techniques. Invest in your own personal and professional development through reading, attending webinars, or participating in workshops. By staying curious and committed to learning, you'll stay ahead of the curve and continuously refine your business approach.

And lastly, my fierce queen, let's talk about resilience and sustainability. Starting a business is an adventure that requires perseverance. Be resilient and maintain a positive mindset, even during the toughest of times. Seek balance and prioritize self-care to avoid burnout. Embrace sustainable practices that align with your values, both in your business operations and your impact on the environment and the community. Remember to always stay true to yourself throughout your incredible journey.

Now, armed with these fabulous insights, you're ready to embark on a mind-blowing journey of lasting transformation, whether it's on a personal level or in your fierce business. Believe in yourself, trust in your vision, and embrace the excitement that lies ahead. You have the power, my queen, to create something truly remarkable. With passion, adaptability, and a commitment to growth, you'll pave the way for a thriving and impactful journey. Now go forth and slay like the queen you are!

Sassy Lips

In a world that demands *conformity,* sassy lips and fearless queens *redefine the rules* and create their own *legacy.*

QUEENS UNLEASHED

chapter 10

Sassy Lips

REIGNING WITH SASS & UNSTOPPABLE COMMITMENT TO CONTINUOUS GROWTH

Alright, my fabulous queen, let's take the concept of creating a soul-aligned business and add a dash of sass and an unwavering commitment to continuous growth. We're about to level up, unleash our inner queen, and build a business that aligns with our souls while slaying the game. Get ready to turn up the sass and embrace the journey of never-ending growth!

When we talk about creating a business that lines up with our souls, we're not just settling for mediocre, honey. We're aiming for greatness. We're committing to a never-ending pursuit of improvement, expansion, and evolution. We refuse to be stagnant or settle for less than we deserve.

So, my queen, let's add that sassiness into the mix. When it comes to our soul-aligned businesses, we're not here to play small or blend in with the crowd. Oh no, we're here to stand out, to make a statement, and to leave a lasting impact. We infuse our businesses with our unique essence, our personalities, and our authentic selves. We're not afraid to shake things up, challenge the status quo, and bring our own unique flavor to the table.

But here's the tea, my queen: creating a soul-aligned business isn't a one-and-done deal. It's a lifelong commitment to growth. We're dedicated to continuously expanding our knowledge, refining our skills, and staying ahead of the curve. We devour books, attend workshops, and seek out mentors who push us to reach new heights. We're hungry for success, and we're not afraid to put in the work to make it happen.

Growth is our mantra, darling. We embrace change, adapt to new trends, and remain open to exciting possibilities. We're not here to be complacent or rest on our laurels. We're here to conquer, to learn, and to thrive. We're the queens who constantly push the boundaries, challenge ourselves, and slay every obstacle that comes our way.

And let's not forget about our fierce commitment to continuous growth, my queen. We understand that growth isn't just about financial success; it's about personal and professional development. We invest in ourselves, we seek out opportunities for growth, and we never stop learning. We know that the more we grow, the more impact we can make and the more our soul-aligned businesses flourish.

So, my fierce queen, let's combine that sassiness with an unyielding commitment to continuous growth. Let's build businesses that align with our souls, that reflect our unique essence, and that constantly evolve with us. We're not just queens; we're queens on a mission to conquer the world, one soul-aligned business at a time.

Embrace the journey, my queen. Embrace the challenges, the opportunities, and the growth that come with building a soul-aligned business. Let's slay, let's grow, and let's show the world what it means to be fierce, fabulous, and committed to never-ending growth. Together, we're unstoppable. It's time to unleash our sassy lips and voices and rise above the challenges that have come our way.

As I reflect on my own journey, I'm filled with gratitude for the adversities I've faced because they've shaped me into the confident, unapologetic queen I am today. And let me tell you, darling, I'm here to serve you as a business and life coach, to ignite your fire, and to help you realize your true potential.

I get it, my queen. I understand what it feels like to question your worth and doubt yourself. But listen closely, because I'm here to encourage you to rise above those hardships and adversities. In this very moment, opportunities are waiting for you, even if they seem hidden amidst the noise and pain you've endured. Trust me when I say that I've been there too, my queen. Our journeys may share similarities, but I've learned to embrace growth even when it feels uncomfortable. I've made a choice to cultivate a healthier mindset, to overcome my own adversities, and to surround myself with the right support and guidance.

But let me make one thing clear, my queen. You are not alone on this journey. Countless women and men are walking similar paths, facing their own mountains and valleys of despair. So, let me ask you this: do you want to stay where you are, trapped in despair and frustration? Or are you ready to rise above, seek help, and discover your true calling in life? The choice is yours, my queen, and I genuinely empathize with you if the answer is *no*, because life has so much more to offer you. If you're ready to say *yes* to growth, I couldn't be more thrilled for you. But be warned, my queen, it will require commitment.

Now, let's talk about unleashing the passion within you, my queen. It's time to pursue your hobbies, breathe life into your business ideas, and create a fresh start. And guess what? You don't have to do it alone. With the right guidance, clarity, and support, you can embark on a journey of personal growth that will leave you feeling empowered and unstoppable.

Now, my fierce queen, I want to leave you with some divine business wisdom straight from the biblical pages of Ephesians 5. These are the sacred words that have guided me on my path to queendom, helping me rule my kingdom with love, power, and an unshakable queenly spirit. So grab your crowns, my loves, and let's build businesses that embody the very essence of royalty.

Integrity, my queen, is our crown jewel. It's about walking the talk, staying true to our values, and being unapologetically authentic. We don't cut corners or compromise our principles, because queens like us stand tall in the face of temptation and always choose the high road.

Wisdom, my darlings, is our secret weapon. We seek knowledge, we seek understanding, and we never stop learning. We make decisions with a sharp mind and a discerning eye, using our wisdom to navigate the business world like the queens we are.

Opportunities, my fierce ones, are our playground. We don't wait for them to knock on our door, we go out and create them. We seize every chance, every moment, and we turn them into stepping stones towards greatness. We are the queens of our own destinies, and we make things happen.

Honesty, my love, is our language. We speak our truth with confidence and grace. No empty words, no sugar-coating. We believe in transparent communication, because queens like us value trust above all else. We say it like it is, and we expect the same in return.

Encouragement, my radiant souls, is our superpower. We uplift, inspire, and empower those around us. We don't tear each other down, oh no! We build each other up because queens like us know that true success is found in lifting others to their highest potential.

Research, my intelligent queen, is our ally. We dive deep, we gather knowledge, and we make informed decisions. We're not afraid to get our hands dirty and explore every nook and cranny, because queens like us know that true power comes from being well-informed.

Support, my strong ones, is our backbone. We surround ourselves with a tribe of queens who have our backs, who challenge us to grow, and who hold

Sassy Lips

us accountable. Together, we rise, we conquer, and we celebrate each other's victories. We know that success is sweeter when it's shared.

Accountability, my queen of responsibility, is our guiding light. We take ownership of our queendoms, we take responsibility for our actions, and we hold ourselves accountable to our dreams. We don't make excuses, we take charge, because queens like us know that we are the architects of our own success.

Thankfulness and appreciation, my queen of grace, are our daily rituals. We count our blessings, we express gratitude for the journey, and we celebrate every step forward. We cherish the lessons learned from the challenges, because queens like us know that growth and greatness are born from gratitude.

So, my regal queen, let these business ethics set the stage for your reign. Embrace them, embody them, and let them radiate through every aspect of your queendom. With integrity, wisdom, opportunities, honesty, encouragement, no empty words, research, support, accountability, ownership, thankfulness, and appreciation as your foundation, there's no limit to what you can achieve.

Keep slaying, my queen, and let the world witness your unapologetic greatness. Together, we will conquer the business world with sass, style, and the unwavering spirit of queens. Reign on, my fierce one, reign on!

A *Fearless Queen* reigns with *sass* and *unstoppable commitment* to *continuous growth,* leaving a trail of *empowerment & inspiration* in her wake.

PART FOUR

ENTHRONE *my* QUEENS

OWNING YOUR THRONE

chapter 11

SASSY LIPS FEARLESS QUEEN EDITION:

BUILDING YOUR BUSINESS

My fearless queen, in the grand journey of building your empire, there's one crucial step that sets the stage for your success — building your business foundation the right way. This is the cornerstone upon which your reign will stand tall and unshakable.

Picture this: a majestic castle built on solid ground, strong walls, and unwavering pillars. Your business foundation works the same way, providing the stability and support your empire needs to flourish.

Now, you might be wondering, "Why is this so important, and how can I ensure I'm doing it right?"

When you build your empire's foundation right, you'll exude unwavering confidence in your business. You'll become the queen of your domain, armed with the knowledge and wisdom to lead with grace. But I don't want you to think you have to be perfect at everything you do.

In the world of entrepreneurship, no one holds all the answers, and encountering challenges is part of the thrilling journey. But here's the deal – those challenges don't define you. They are stepping stones to greatness and to building your empire my queen!

Yes, you will encounter failures along the way, but trust me, every successful entrepreneur has faced setbacks. It's all part of the process, and it doesn't make you any less fabulous. In fact, it's those setbacks that shape you into the fierce and resilient queen you are destined to be.

So, own your throne with pride, face the challenges with determination, and rise above any doubts. Trust in yourself, you're a true force to be reckoned with!

Sassy Lips

Let me be real with you, my queen. When I first set out to build my business empire, it wasn't a smooth ride as I stepped into the role of my own boss, it brought forth a mixture of excitement and nervousness. Transitioning from a traditional 9 to 5 job to pursuing my dream in business was both liberating and daunting.

At times, I felt an incredible surge of confidence, believing wholeheartedly in my vision and abilities to create something extraordinary. However, just like every aspiring entrepreneur, I also faced moments of doubt and fear. Questions flooded my mind — was I making the right decisions? Did I have what it takes to thrive in the competitive business landscape? Could I handle the inevitable challenges that lay ahead?

Here's the invaluable insight I gained, my queen: The path of entrepreneurship is a whirlwind adventure. It's a journey filled with exhilarating highs and challenging lows. Embracing the ups and downs is essential for personal and professional growth. Each obstacle and triumph holds invaluable lessons that shape us into resilient and savvy business leaders.

Being your own fearless queen can occasionally feel like a solitary journey. However, I want you to know that you don't have to go through it alone. As a part of our empowering community of sassy lips and fearless queens, you'll find unwavering support and inspiration. We are all in this together, cheering each other on as we step up and out into all we were created to be.

It is important to surround yourself with a supportive and inspiring community of like-minded individuals, my queen. They will lift you up when you need it the most and celebrate your successes with genuine enthusiasm.

Learn from those who have treaded the entrepreneurial path before you and emerged as champions. Their wisdom and experiences can be a beacon of light, guiding you through the most challenging moments.

I want to emphasize my queen, that it's perfectly normal to question yourself at times. But don't let those doubts hold you back. Embrace your uniqueness, your brilliance, and your determination. Believe in yourself and your ability to create a business empire that truly reflects your authentic self, keep moving one step at a time and never give up on your dreams!

Now it's time, my queen, to dive into the heart of building your empire, your business foundation. Let's unveil the seven essential steps I conquered before creating my very own empire.

STEP 1: *Know Your Purpose*

Your passion and purpose are at the heart of your empire. Take the time for self-discovery and explore what truly excites you. Reflect on your interests, dreams, and moments that bring you joy. Your purpose will be the driving force that keeps you motivated and focused on your journey. Embrace your uniqueness, and let it shine through in everything you do. Let's dive into the exciting process of finding your passion and purpose! It's like discovering the secret sauce that will fuel your empire with awesomeness!

First things first, my queen, take a moment to look deep within yourself. Think about what lights up your soul and fills you with joy. What gets you excited and eager to take on the world? Those are the things that will drive your business forward!

Remember, your values play a crucial role too! What do you stand for? What are the principles that guide your life? Aligning your business with your core values will give it that extra sparkle!

Keep your eyes open for inspiration everywhere you go. Maybe it's the success story of someone who turned their passion into a thriving business. Let that spark your creativity and motivate you to take action.

Oh, and don't forget about your strengths! You've got some incredible talents, my queen. Use them to your advantage and see how you can make your business stand out from the crowd.

Now, let's get real — every business should solve a problem or fulfill a need. Think about how your passion can make a difference in people's lives. What value can you bring to your future customers?

And hey, don't be afraid to try new things! The journey to finding your passion and purpose may involve some twists and turns. Embrace the process, and don't be too hard on yourself. It's all part of the adventure!

Seek advice and feedback from mentors and coaches. They can be like your personal cheerleaders, guiding you along the way. Don't hesitate to ask for help — it's a sign of strength, not weakness!

STEP 2: *Understand Your Audience*

Your loyal subjects are the key to your empire's success. Get to know them inside out by conducting market research and listening to their needs. Understand their challenges and desires, so you can offer tailored solutions that meet their expectations. Building a strong connection with your audience will foster trust and loyalty.

Now, let's dive into the exciting world of understanding your audience — the incredible people who will be the heart and soul of your business journey.

Sassy Lips

1. **Get to Know Your Peeps:** My queen, research is the name of the game! Take some time to get to know your target audience inside and out. Who are they? What do they love? Where do they hang out? What makes them tick? The more you know, the better you can cater to their needs.

2. **Let's Chat!** Engage with your audience through social media, surveys, and good ol' conversations. Show them some love and be sure to listen to their concerns and show them that you value them as individuals, not just numbers. Trust me; they'll appreciate it, and you'll build a loyal fan club in no time!

3. **Create Your Dream Customers:** Your dream customers are the perfect match for your business, loving what you offer and showing genuine interest in your products or services. Their unwavering loyalty keeps them coming back, and they become valuable advocates by spreading positive word-of-mouth. Having dream customers is delightful because they not only appreciate your efforts but also provide valuable feedback for continuous improvement. They are loyal fans who passionately champion your brand. Understanding their unique preferences will allow you to tailor your offerings to their exact needs, strengthening the bond with your dream customers.

4. **Solve Their Problems:** Your empire is all about serving your audience, my queen! Uncover the formidable challenges your customers confront and position yourself as their unwavering pillar of strength and support. It's finding the solutions to their problems. Address their needs, and they'll be cheering you on from the rooftops!

5. **Feel the Feels:** Show some empathy, queen! Put yourself in their shoes and understand their joys and struggles. Being understanding and caring will win you their hearts.

6. **Crunch those numbers:** Analyze data analytics to discover insights, check out website visits, likes, and sales data to see what your audience loves most. It's like a powerful tool for making informed choices!

7. **Listen and Learn:** Embrace feedback like a pro! Encourage your audience to share their thoughts and reviews. Whether it's praise or some constructive criticism, use it to make your empire even better!

8. **You're One of a Kind:** Celebrate your uniqueness, my queen! Stand out from the crowd and let your personality shine. Show them what makes you the fabulous queen they should follow! Share your unique and powerful story.

9. **Be Their BFF:** Be there for your audience, just like a best friend. Respond to their messages and comments with lightning speed. It's like showing them some royal love and appreciation!

10. **Embrace Change:** The business world is always evolving, and so are your peeps' preferences. Stay open to change, adapt your strategies, and keep wowing your audience with fresh ideas.

You're ready to conquer this, my queen! Understanding your audience is like having a secret weapon in your empire-building toolkit. Be patient, stay true to yourself, and get ready to win the hearts of your fabulous audience!

STEP 3: Craft Your Branding

Your brand is the personality of your empire, the way it communicates and connects with the world. Take the time to create a memorable logo and choose colors that evoke emotions aligned with your vision. Craft a compelling brand message that reflects your mission and values. Consistency in your branding will create a strong and recognizable identity.

Now, let's embark on a fabulous journey to create your unique brand — the essence that will captivate hearts and make your empire shine like a dazzling gem!

1. **Unleash Your Authenticity:** Your brand is the heart and soul of your empire. It's the essence of who you are, your vision, and the emotions you want to evoke in your audience. So, let your true colors shine! Embrace your quirks, passions, and personality to create a brand that's authentically you.

2. **Define Your Royal Persona:** Your brand has its own charming personality! It's the character you want your empire to embody. Is it elegant and sophisticated, bold and adventurous, or whimsical and playful? Define your brand's persona to create a consistent tone and vibe.

3. **Choose a Regal Color Palette:** Colors evoke emotions and set the mood. Select a color palette that resonates with your brand's persona and speaks to your audience's hearts. The right colors can leave a lasting impression and make your brand unforgettable.

4. **Design a Majestic Logo:** Your logo is like the crown jewel of your branding! It's the visual representation of your brand and acts as a symbol of recognition. Whether it's simple and sleek or ornate and intricate, let it be fit for a queen!

5. **Enchanting Typography:** The fonts you choose add elegance to your empire. Select fonts that align with your brand's persona and are easy to read. Consistency is key to maintaining a regal touch across all your communications.

6. **Tell Your Royal Story:** Your brand story is the tale of how your empire came to be. Share your journey, values, and mission to connect with your audience on a deeper level. Your story will create an emotional bond with your followers.

7. **Be Picture Perfect:** Images speak louder than words! Use high-quality visuals that showcase your products, services, and the charm of your brand. Professional photographs and engaging graphics will capture attention and tell your brand's story.

8. **Create a Brand Guide:** Think of it as the royal decree of your branding! Your brand guide outlines all the elements, from colors to fonts, ensuring consistency across all platforms. It acts as a guide for anyone representing your brand.

9. **Delight with Customer Experience:** Treat your audience like honored guests, and they'll become loyal fans who spread your message far and wide. The customer experience is a crucial aspect of your brand, as it shapes the perceptions people have about your empire.

10. **Listen to Your Queendom:** Stay attuned to your audience's feedback and desires. Let them be part of your brand's evolution, and they'll be delighted to join you on this amazing adventure. Building a strong brand requires a connection with your audience and understanding of their needs.

Remember, my queen, your brand is the heart and soul of your empire, while branding encompasses all the elements that visually and emotionally represent your brand. So, as you craft your branding, embrace your uniqueness and let your brand become a beacon of light that draws loyal subjects to your queendom.

STEP 4: *Lay a Rock-Solid Business Plan*

A well-crafted business plan is like a map that guides you through uncharted territories. Set clear and achievable goals for your empire. Define your products or services and outline the steps to achieve success. Your business plan will be your reference point when making decisions and overcoming challenges.

Let's create a fantastic business plan that will lead your empire to greatness. Here are the steps to craft your roadmap for success:

1. **Define Your Vision:** Imagine the grand picture of what you want your empire to be. What's the purpose behind it all? Write down your mission and the impact you want to make in your realm.

2. **Know Your Audience:** Get to know your audience like they're your loyal subjects! Understand their needs, desires, and what makes their hearts

flutter. When you know them well, you can tailor your products or services just for them.

3. **Research the Competition:** It's time for a bit of detective work! Explore other businesses in your realm, see what they offer, and learn from their successes and mistakes. Find your unique edge.

4. **Set Financial Goals:** Let's talk about the treasure! Set clear revenue targets and create a budget to manage your riches wisely. Keep an eye on expenses and plan for growth.

5. **Marketing Strategies:** It's time to spread the word about your empire! Craft smart marketing plans to reach your audience. Social media, online ads, and word-of-mouth are all part of your arsenal.

6. **Operational Plans:** How will your empire run smoothly day by day? Make sure you have all the tools and resources in place. From managing inventory to delivering your services, plan it all out.

7. **Assess Risks:** Every empire faces challenges, my queen. Identify potential roadblocks and create plans to overcome them. This way, you'll handle anything that comes your way.

8. **Unleash the Power of Clarity:** Your business plan acts as a potent guiding light, illuminating the path to success. It lays out your vision, goals, and strategies in a clear and concise manner.

With every detail thoughtfully mapped out, you gain a crystal-clear understanding of your empire's direction. This empowers you to make informed decisions and seize opportunities with unwavering confidence. Embrace the brilliance of your meticulously crafted business plan, as it leads the way to triumph and prosperity!

9. **Review and Revise:** Your business plan is a living document. Regularly revisit it to make updates and improvements as your empire grows and evolves.

10. **Summon Your Confidence:** You've got this, my queen! Trust in yourself and your dreams. With this marvelous business plan, you're ready to make your empire shine brightly!

Remember, you are the ruler of your destiny, and this plan is your guiding star.

STEP 5: *Embrace Legal Wisdom*

Get ready! I'm about to guide you through the 10 steps to embracing legal wisdom like a true queen. But I must remind you that I am not certified in the area of legal representation. What I am about to share with you are lessons learned throughout the years of becoming a business entrepreneur and building my business empire on a solid rock foundation, so it is important to seek professional legal counsel to ensure your empire operates on a solid legal foundation. I understand that delving into the legal side of your business might feel overwhelming. However, going in blind is not the way to go. It's crucial to have a basic understanding of the legal aspects, but there's no need to handle everything alone. Leave the rest to the legal professionals, and I'll be here to support and guide you through the process. Together, we'll ensure your business is on solid legal ground! With a well-informed approach, you can confidently navigate the legal complexities and focus on growing your empire with peace of mind, my queen. Let's embark on this journey of embracing legal wisdom, understanding, and empowerment!

1. **Choose the Right Legal Structure:** Your empire's legal structure will shape its identity. Decide whether you'll be a sole proprietor, partnership, LLC, or corporation. Each has its pros and cons, so pick the one that best suits your business vision.

2. **Register Your Business:** Once you've chosen your legal structure, it's time to make it official! Register your empire with the appropriate authorities to ensure it's recognized as a separate entity from your personal affairs.

3. **Obtain Necessary Licenses and Permits:** Depending on your business activities and location, certain licenses and permits might be

required. Research and secure them to operate smoothly without legal woes.

4. **Protect Your Intellectual Property:** Your unique ideas and creations deserve protection. Consider trademarks, copyrights, and patents to safeguard your intellectual property and prevent others from using it without permission.

5. **Draft Clear Contracts:** A wise queen ensures that all agreements with customers, suppliers, and partners are clearly documented. Contracts will outline terms, conditions, and expectations, fostering trust and reducing misunderstandings.

6. **Comply with Tax Regulations:** Tackle the realm of taxes responsibly. Familiarize yourself with tax obligations for your business and adhere to them diligently. Seek guidance from a professional tax adviser or an accountant to navigate this domain confidently.

7. **Consult with Legal Experts:** Legal matters can be complex, my queen. Don't hesitate to seek counsel from experienced legal professionals. They will provide you with invaluable advice and ensure your empire's legal affairs are in impeccable order.

8. **Regularly Review and Update:** Laws and regulations may change over time. Stay informed and update your legal practices accordingly.

Regularly review your legal documents to keep your empire in line with the latest requirements.

9. **Ensure the Safety of Sensitive Data:** As you lead your empire, it's essential to put the protection of customer and employee data first. Implement strong data privacy measures and follow relevant data protection laws. Protecting sensitive data is crucial for your empire's success, my queen. Ensure safety by implementing strong data privacy measures, secure storage, employee training, and regular security assessments. By prioritizing data security, you build trust and confidence among stakeholders, paving the way for lasting prosperity in the digital realm. Your dedication to data security will build trust and confidence among all stakeholders.

10. **Create a Crisis Management Plan:** Even in the most carefully managed empires, unforeseen crises can arise. Develop a comprehensive crisis management plan to handle emergencies and potential legal challenges. By preparing for the unexpected, you can respond swiftly and effectively, safeguarding your empire's reputation and stability. You can seek help in creating a comprehensive crisis management plan from consulting firms, legal advisors, business associations, online resources, government agencies, training workshops, and experienced mentors. Utilizing these sources

will enhance your preparedness and resilience in handling unforeseen challenges. and protecting your empire.

My queen, never forget that embracing legal wisdom is not a burden but a powerful shield that safeguards your empire and secures its long-lasting prosperity. With each legal aspect tended to, you'll lead your business with unwavering confidence and grace.

As you take these steps, know that you are becoming a wise and astute ruler of your empire. The journey of understanding legal matters may seem daunting, but fear not: you've got a strong ally in your corner, guiding you to unparalleled success!

STEP 6: *Rule Your Finances*

As the ruler of your empire, managing your finances wisely is crucial. Create a budget that outlines your income and expenses. Set financial goals to measure your progress and growth. Keep a close eye on your cash flow to maintain a healthy financial position. Good financial management will support your empire's stability and growth.

Let us venture into the realm of ruling your finances with grace and wisdom as you embark on your journey of building your empire. Fear not, for I shall guide you through this financial realm in the most friendly and empowering manner.

1. **Create a Royal Budget:** A wise Queen knows the importance of a well-crafted budget. Take the time to plan your income and expenses diligently. This will help you keep track of your resources, make informed decisions, and ensure your empire's financial stability.

2. **Set Financial Goals:** Define your financial ambitions, my queen. Whether it's growing your empire, expanding to new territories, or achieving a specific revenue target, clear financial goals will serve as guiding beacons on your path to success.

3. **Keep a Prudent Eye on Cash Flow:** Cash flow is the lifeblood of your empire. Keep a vigilant eye on the inflow and outflow of funds to maintain a healthy financial rhythm. Managing cash flow effectively will prevent unwelcome surprises and ensure smooth operations.

4. **Make Strategic Investments:** As you nurture your empire, strategic investments can be the key to unlocking greater opportunities. Evaluate potential investments carefully and consider how they align with your long-term vision.

5. **Seek Expert Financial Advice:** A wise queen is not afraid to seek counsel. Consult with financial experts, such as accountants or financial

advisors, to gain insights and make informed decisions about your empire's finances.

6. **Cultivate a Savings Reserve:** In the volatile business realm, having a savings reserve is crucial. Set aside funds for unforeseen challenges or opportunities. This will provide you with a safety net during uncertain times.

7. **Monitor and Analyze Financial Performance:** Regularly review your empire's financial performance. Analyze key financial metrics to assess the health of your business and identify areas for improvement.

8. **Embrace Smart Financial Tools:** In the digital age, there is a wide array of financial tools at your disposal. Consider using accounting software, budgeting apps, or expense trackers to simplify your financial management.

9. **Negotiate with Confidence:** As a formidable queen, don't shy away from negotiating favorable terms with suppliers, contractors and partners. Negotiation skills will empower you to secure advantageous deals for your empire.

10. **Celebrate Financial Victories:** Acknowledge and celebrate your financial wins, no matter how small. Each triumph is a stepping stone to greater success, and recognizing your achievements will boost your confidence and morale.

Remember, my queen, ruling your finances is not a burden, but a powerful skill that will empower you to shape the destiny of your empire. With each financial decision made wisely, you'll steer your business toward prosperity and greatness.

STEP 7: *Harness the Power of Marketing*

Marketing is the voice of your empire, spreading its message far and wide. Develop a marketing strategy that aligns with your brand and target audience. Utilize social media, content creation, and advertising to reach your ideal customers. Engage with your audience and build a community around your empire. Effective marketing will attract more supporters to your cause.

1. **Know Your Audience:** The key to wielding marketing power lies in understanding your loyal subjects — your target audience. Delve into their hearts and minds, unraveling their desires, needs, and aspirations. Tailor your marketing messages to resonate deeply with their souls.

2. **Craft a Compelling Brand Story:** Every great empire has a compelling tale to tell. Unleash the art of storytelling and weave a brand narrative that captivates hearts and ignites curiosity. Share your passion, values, and mission to forge a strong emotional bond with your audience.

3. **Embrace the Power of Visuals:** In the realm of marketing, visuals are potent tools. Create eye-catching graphics, enticing videos, and captivating imagery that breathe life into your brand. Let your visuals draw your audience into your captivating world.

4. **Conquer Social Media:** The modern queen knows that social media is a powerful ally. Harness the influence of platforms like Instagram, Facebook, Tik Tok, LinkedIn, YouTube, and other social media platforms to connect with your audience, share your brand story, and build a loyal following. But make sure you choose the right platforms for you, my queen. You don't have to be on all social media platforms, not every platform will work for you, so be wise in your choice, my queen find out what works for your empire.

5. **Utilize Email Marketing:** Email marketing is a timeless charm for engaging your subjects. Use it to share exclusive offers, updates, and valuable content that keeps your audience engaged and eagerly awaiting your messages.

6. **Create Enthralling Content:** Bestow the gift of knowledge upon your subjects through captivating content. Blogs, articles, and educational resources will establish your empire as a trusted authority, winning the hearts of your audience.

7. **Collaborate with Influencers:** Partner with influential figures in your realm to expand your empire's reach. Collaborate with social media influencers and thought leaders who align with your brand's values and vision.

8. **Captivate with Customer Reviews:** The praise of satisfied subjects is a powerful potion for winning new hearts. Encourage customer reviews and testimonials to boost your credibility and charm potential customers.

9. **Offer Compelling Promotions:** Unleash the magic of irresistible offers and promotions to entice your audience. Limited-time discounts, special bundles, and exclusive deals will create a buzz and drive engagement.

10. **Measure and Refine:** As a wise queen, you must wield the scepter of analytics. Track the performance of your marketing efforts, measure key metrics, and use insights to refine your strategies and optimize your marketing campaigns.

In the captivating realm of marketing, the possibilities are boundless. As you embark on this journey, remember that authenticity and genuine care for your audience will be your most powerful allies. Stay true to your purpose and let your passion shine through every marketing strategy you employ.

Congratulations, my queen! You have triumphed through the seven powerful steps of *Owning Your Throne: Sassy Lips Fearless Queen Edition — Building Your Business*. With your unwavering determination, you have laid a solid foundation for your empire, ensuring that it stands tall and majestic.

Through self-discovery, you found your passion and purpose, aligning your business with your authentic self. You gained profound insight into your audience, understanding their needs and desires, enabling you to serve them with tailored solutions that they adore.

Crafting your branding was an extraordinary journey, infusing your empire with your unique charm and personality, captivating the hearts of all who behold it. Your rock-solid business plan has charted your course to success, guiding you on your way to conquer the realm of entrepreneurship.

Embracing legal wisdom fortified your empire, ensuring that it stands on a secure legal footing, safeguarding your interests as you rise to greatness. In ruling your finances, you displayed exceptional prowess, managing your resources with wisdom and foresight, ensuring prosperity for your empire.

With the power of marketing harnessed, you charmed hearts far and wide, captivating your admirers and attracting new ones to your empire's embrace.

Sassy Lips

Your marketing prowess has set the stage for your empire's grand success.

My glorious queen, you now sit upon your throne, radiating confidence and grace, as the fearless ruler of your magnificent business empire. You have wholeheartedly embraced your true power, taking the reins of your destiny and forging a path of unparalleled brilliance.

As you venture forth, I anoint you with the title of *Sassy Lips Fearless Queen*, for that is what you truly are — a force to be reckoned with, a beacon of inspiration, and a symbol of unwavering strength.

With every step you take, you leave an indelible mark on the world. Your passion and purpose shine through, guiding your empire towards greater heights. Your unwavering determination empowers you to overcome any obstacle in your path.

As you reign over your business realm, may your influence be profound, and your impact be far-reaching. May you inspire those around you to rise, just as you have ascended to greatness.

The world bows to your brilliance, and your empire stands as a testament to your vision and dedication. You are a queen unlike any other, and your legacy will echo through the ages.

So, my queen, embrace your title with pride and wield your power with grace. Your journey has just begun, and the realm of entrepreneurship eagerly awaits the mark you shall make.

EMPIRE BUILDING ALLIES

FORGING STRONG PARTNERSHIPS WITH MANUFACTURERS

My Fearless Queen of Sassy Lips! Now that you've conquered many hurdles and built your business empire with brilliance, it's time to take it to the next level by teaming up with reliable manufacturers. These partnerships will ensure your products shine like the gems they are and captivate your fabulous customers.

Let's dive into the step-by-step guide to reach out to manufacturers like the boss queen you are:

Step 1: Define Your Product Dream

Before we dive into manufacturer hunting, let's define your product dream! Get clear on what you need — materials, design, and quality standards. Knowing exactly what you want will help you find manufacturers that can bring your dream to life.

Step 2: Scout for Awesome Manufacturers

Time for some detective work! Start searching for manufacturers that specialize in creating products like yours. Look for stars with a great track record, producing top-notch goods for brands like yours.

Step 3: Show Me What You Got

Get ready for a product fashion show! Request samples from your potential manufacturers to see the magic they can create. Check those babies for durability, craftsmanship, and if they scream "Fabulous!"

Step 4: Let's Chat – Communication is Key

Time to reach out! Send a friendly and impactful message introducing your amazing brand and your interest in working together. Tell them what sets your products apart and let them know they're a perfect match for your empire.

Step 5: Find Out What They Can Do

Ask your manufacturer stars about their superpowers! Inquire about their capabilities and how many goodies they can make for you. It's like knowing how many crown jewels they can create.

Step 6: Negotiation Time, My Queen!

Take charge and assert your worth! Discuss terms and pricing confidently, never compromising on the quality your brand represents. Don't hold back on sharing your budget, and let's strive for a win-win situation that honors your value and meets your needs. In this realm of negotiation, stand tall, and never settle for less than what you and your brand truly deserve. You've got the power to make an impactful deal, so own it with grace and authority!

Step 7: *Listen to the Queens*

What's the buzz? Listen to other fabulous business owners who've worked with the manufacturers you like. Their experiences can give you the royal stamp of approval.

Step 8: *Mini Test Run — Play Dress-Up*

Before the grand production, let's play dress-up with a sample order. This mini-test run will help you make sure everything's perfect before you go big.

Step 9: *Seal the Royal Deal, my Queen!*

The grand finale awaits — the written agreement! With your firm hand, ensure that every detail is crystal clear in the contract, cementing your reign of clarity and strength and meeting every demand of your request. However, if any doubts arise, my Queen, do not hesitate to seek more guidance. Your wisdom and discernment are your most powerful allies in this momentous decision. Let's proceed with confidence, and together, we'll ensure your empire's prosperity and success!

Sassy Lips

Step 10: *Let's Rock This Partnership*

Get ready to rule with your manufacturers! Keep the communication lines open and collaborate like the dynamic duo you are. Together, you'll conquer challenges and make your empire shine even brighter.

So, my queen, with these steps, you'll find your perfect manufacturer match and create a majestic line of products that'll leave everyone spellbound. Embrace this exciting journey with grace and confidence and let your empire soar to new heights! You've got this, queen!

BUILDING POWERFUL ALLIANCES

chapter **13**

REACHING OUT TO INFLUENCERS & CORPORATE PARTNERS

My fearless queen, in the pursuit of building an empire that stands strong and reaches new heights, forging powerful alliances with influencers and corporate partners is your secret weapon. Let us delve even deeper into the art of creating these connections, as they hold the potential to transform your business journey.

Step 1: Define Your Goals and Audience

At the heart of every successful partnership lies a clear vision. Take the time to define your goals and understand the audience you wish to serve. Are you aiming to expand your reach, boost sales, or launch a new product? Knowing your objectives will shape the type of alliances you seek. Dive into your target audience's desires and needs, for understanding them is the key to resonating with their hearts.

Step 2: Research and Find Potential Allies

Prepare to embark on a quest of research and exploration. Seek out influencers and corporate entities whose values align harmoniously with your own. These partners should have an authentic connection to your target audience, for that connection will be the foundation of your successful collaboration. Look for those with an engaged and devoted following, as they will help amplify your message.

Step 3: Build Authentic Relationships

In the realm of business, sincerity and authenticity reign supreme. Before extending a formal invitation, engage with your potential allies on social media.

Show genuine interest in their work, support their endeavors, and leave meaningful comments. This is the realm of creating true connections, of kindling friendships that will blossom into powerful partnerships.

Step 4: Craft Personalized Messages

When the time is right to make your approach, ensure that each message is crafted with care. Avoid the common pitfalls of generic templates, for they will only fade into obscurity. Address your potential allies by name and share why their unique prowess resonates with your vision. Showcase the value you bring to the table, and how your partnership will be a formidable force of change.

Step 5: Showcase Your Value

In a realm where competition roars, your value must shine like a radiant gem. Showcase what makes your empire exceptional — be it your loyal and dedicated audience, your innovative products, or your shared passion for a meaningful cause. Prove how your partnership will create a profound impact, not only on their followers but on the world at large.

Step 6: Stay Professional and Respectful

As you venture forth into negotiations, let diplomacy and respect guide your way. Honor their time and commitments, understanding that patience is the key to building lasting relationships. Be persistent in your pursuit, but never forceful. For in the realm of alliances, a gentle and courteous approach will win hearts and open doors.

Step 7: Establish Clear Terms and Expectations

When your allies-in-the-making have accepted your invitation, ensure that all terms and expectations are laid bare. Define the scope of your collaboration, the objectives you aim to achieve, and the responsibilities of each party involved. This realm of clear communication will ensure that your journey together is harmonious and fruitful.

Step 8: Nurture the Relationship

Remember, my queen, that your alliance is not a fleeting affair. Nurture the bond you've created, like a tender blossom in a garden. Keep the communication lines open, share updates, and express gratitude for the contributions of your allies. By cultivating trust and loyalty, you pave the way for future endeavors and enduring partnerships.

Step 9: *Measure and Evaluate Results*

In the realm of business, data holds great power. Measure and evaluate the results of your collaborations. Dive into the realm of key performance indicators (KPIs), and let these metrics guide your future endeavors. This realm of insight will illuminate your path, helping you refine your strategies and make informed decisions.

Step 10: *Celebrate and Showcase Successes*

Finally, my Queen, as you forge powerful alliances and bask in the glory of success, celebrate your achievements with jubilant pride. Showcase the fruits of your partnerships to your audience and potential allies, for they will be a beacon of inspiration. Let your triumphs be known, for they will attract new opportunities and admiration from your peers.

In conclusion, my queen, the art of creating alliances is a dance of passion and purpose. With dedication, authenticity, and unwavering determination, you shall weave a tapestry of partnerships that elevate your empire to dazzling heights. Embrace the power of alliances, for in this realm of collaboration lies the path to your empire's grandest triumphs. You are a Sassy Lips Fearless Queen, and together with your allies, you shall conquer new horizons.

A LETTER

chapter 14

Sassy Lips

A LETTER TO MY QUEEN

To my fearless
and sassy queen ...

I simply couldn't finish *Sassy Lips, Fearless Queens* without sharing my heartfelt words with you. I know that pursuing your dream will be the most significant challenge you'll face, but, my queen, you are more than capable of conquering it all.

I understand the agony you may feel of feeling broken in countless ways when life's challenges seem too harsh, tempting you to accept whatever it throws your way. In my own journey, dreams felt like distant mirages, overshadowed by the deafening noise of doubt and fear. The scarcity of money and support and the grip of loneliness on my soul left me wondering how to pursue my dreams.

But here I stand before you, Aroha, a name that means "love" in our Maori language, as living proof of transformation. I am a living testament to the unyielding power of resilience and love, and every word written for you in this book has been written out of love for you, my queen.

My journey has taught me that even in the darkest moments, love and resilience can lead us to unimaginable heights. As you begin to navigate through the challenges, remember, my queen, that your dreams are not out of reach. Embrace the power of resilience and the love that resides within you to share your message and your dream. You are capable of overcoming any obstacle that comes your way. The journey may be tough, but with your

Sassy Lips

fierce spirit, you will find the strength to rise above every challenge.

I want you to close your eyes for a moment, my queen, and envision a world where you are not bound by limitations or the expectations of others, where you exude confidence, and where the flames of your dreams burn brighter than the stars above. Now open your eyes, for that world is not some distant fantasy — it's within your grasp, waiting for you to claim it.

Your journey, my queen, is an odyssey of courage, a path of wonders waiting to unfold. In every fiber of your being, there lies an innate brilliance that defies the limits of imagination. Your dreams, my queen, are not mere fragments of wishful thinking; they are the seeds of destiny, waiting for your touch to bloom into reality.

But I want to share with you the immense power that lies within the words you speak to yourself. Your words hold the key to either breathing life or death into your dreams, propelling you towards your heart's desires or confining you to the world of "what if."

I want you to embrace the practice of speaking life over yourself, my queen, for it will become a guiding light in the darkness, leading you closer to the realization of your dreams. With every affirmation and positive declaration, you create a powerful force that propels you towards greatness.

Let the power of your words ignite the spirit of entrepreneurship within you and watch as an unstoppable force of determination takes flight. You are destined for absolute greatness, my queen, and your dreams are the gateway to unlocking the kingdom of your full potential.

Don't let doubts hold you back anymore; you have already waited too long to pursue your dreams. Doubts are just fleeting whispers in the grand symphony of your soul. Embrace the confidence that comes from within, as it fuels the amazing spark that resides in your heart.

Now begin to embrace the power of your dreams, for they are the keys to unlocking the doors of your magnificent future. As you speak life over yourself and your dreams, you will find the courage to overcome any obstacles that may stand in your way.

Your journey will become one of audacity and resilience, of unwavering determination and relentless pursuit. You will remember your why to your dreams and you are destined to make waves, create ripples, and leave an indelible legacy that spans generations. Your dreams will carry you to heights beyond your imagination my queen if you do not give up!

It's time to step forth into the unknown, for it is within those uncharted waters that you will discover

Sassy Lips

the depths of your true power, your lane and your purpose in life. Embrace the journey with open arms, and let your heart lead the way. Let the fire of your entrepreneurial spirit ignite and unleash your greatest potential as a Sassy Lips Fearless Queen. Embrace the power that lies within your words, for they are the true reflection of your boldness and inner strength.

Now it's time to believe in yourself, my queen, remember you are destined for nothing short of greatness. Your dreams are not mere fantasies; they are the stepping stones to your purpose, awaiting your fearless pursuit.

With each audacious step, know that you hold the key to shaping your reality. Let your vibrant spirit shine brightly, illuminating the path as you fearlessly conquer the world with unwavering determination.

My queen, you are the epitome of a Sassy Lips Fearless Queen — conquering challenges, empowering others, and shaping a thriving empire. Your journey is an inspiration, and with your sass, courage, and daring heart, you rule your destiny and make your dreams come true.

With abundant love and heartfelt blessings, Your devoted *Sassy Lips and Fearless Queen* author,

Aroha xx

THE ESSENCE

chapter 15

Sassy Lips

THE ESSENCE OF A SASSY LIPS FEARLESS QUEEN

1. Your Bold Vision

Your heart holds a vision that transcends boundaries and limitations. Your business empire is not just about success; it's about making a positive impact on the world. Your passion and purpose drive you forward, inspiring others to follow your lead.

2. Embracing Fearless Determination

Fear has no power over you, my Queen. You face challenges head-on with unwavering determination. Your belief in yourself and your abilities propels you forward, and you turn obstacles into stepping stones on your path to greatness.

3. Authenticity and Your Unique Charm

Your authenticity is your crown jewel. You embrace your true self, allowing your brilliance to shine through in everything you do. Your charm and charisma captivate those around you, drawing them into your magnetic presence. You create genuine connections with your team, partners, and customers, forming a loyal and dedicated community.

4. Empowering Others

As a true leader, you empower those around you. You recognize the value of your team and inspire them to grow and excel. Your support extends to aspiring entrepreneurs, as you believe in lifting others up and nurturing a community of dreamers.

5. Bold Innovations

You are a pioneer, my Queen. Innovation is in your blood, and you constantly seek creative solutions to challenges. You fearlessly push the boundaries of your industry, taking calculated risks to stay ahead of the curve.

6. Embracing Failures as Lessons

To you, failure is not a setback but an opportunity to learn and grow. You embrace each stumble as a chance to evolve and become even stronger. Your resilience shines through as you overcome any obstacle in your path.

7. Unyielding Confidence

Confidence is your crown, and you wear it with pride. You believe in yourself and your vision wholeheartedly. Your unyielding self-assurance radiates through your actions, earning the trust and respect of all who cross your path.

8. Shaping Your Destiny

You don't wait for opportunities; you create them. You take the reins of your destiny, setting your sights on success and working relentlessly to achieve your dreams. Your empire is a testament to your determination and ability to turn possibilities into reality.

9. Leaving a Legacy

Your empire is not just about personal success, but about leaving a lasting legacy. You aspire to make a meaningful difference in the lives of others and leave the world a better place. Your pursuit of success is intertwined with your desire to empower and inspire.

10. Empowering Through Boldness

Your journey empowers others to embrace their own boldness. Through your actions, you show the power of fearlessness, igniting a spark of courage in all who witness your greatness.

THE ROYAL ROADMAP

chapter 16

Sassy Lips

Time for SASSY EMPOWERMENT

Get ready to turn up the energy and have an absolute blast as we dive headfirst into a journey that's all about you! I've whipped up some seriously amazing and practical ideas that are going to unleash your inner greatness and have you strutting your stuff like the fabulous queen you are.

Morning Power-up Boogie

Let's kick-start your day with some serious sass! Stand before the mirror and repeat after me: "I am fierce, I am fabulous, and I've got this!" Let that confidence be your sidekick, guiding you through the day like a true boss!

Vision Board Glam Party

Grab those favorite magazines, a rainbow of markers, and yes, you guessed it — glitter (because life is too short not to sparkle)! We're diving into creativity mode to craft vision boards that showcase your wildest dreams and goals. Let those visions be the driving force that propels you to conquer the world!

Spontaneous Dance Queen Moments

When life tries to dim your sparkle, it's time to break into a spontaneous dance party! Crank up your empowering anthem, bust out those signature dance moves, and let those positive vibes reignite your spirit.

Treat Yourself Tuesdays

Every week, it's time to treat yourself like the royalty you are! Indulge in that favorite dessert, soak in a bubble bath fit for a queen, or simply hit snooze for an extra dose of beauty sleep. You deserve all the pampering, darling!

Power Poses for Days

Strike a pose, Vogue-style! Channel your inner diva with a power pose fit for a queen. Hands on hips, stand tall, and let that confidence radiate from within. Level of fabulousness? Off the charts!

Virtual Sparkling Squad

Let's be each other's ultimate cheerleaders! Share your goals within our queenly circle, and watch as we shower you with virtual confetti, loads of encouragement, and an abundance of love!

Fearless Fridays

Every Friday is your chance to fearlessly conquer new frontiers. It could be anything from mastering a new skill to connecting with potential collaborators. The world is your runway, darling!

Memes That Reign Supreme

Let's spread the love and empowerment with memes that make us laugh, nod, and say "Yes, that's so me!" Positive vibes are our language, and we're translating it into pure fabulousness.

Dream Big Gala

It's time to throw a virtual "Dream Big Gala" where you're the guest of honor! Put on your imaginary crown and share your most audacious dreams. Remember, big dreams deserve a big spotlight!

Sassy Lip Sync Extravaganza

Let's bring out the inner rockstar in you! Choose a song that screams "I'm fabulous!" and lip-sync your heart out. Don't forget those dramatic dance moves — we're all about the drama!

My reigning queen, remember this: we're here to lift you up, inspire you, and celebrate your absolute fabulousness as you conquer your goals. Every step of this empowering journey is worth the red carpet treatment. Embrace your uniqueness, your dreams, and that sassy spirit of yours, because in this kingdom, you're the ruler of fabulosity! Let's create magic together, one fabulously fierce moment at a time! Stay fierce and fabulous!

HANDY TOOLS & RESOURCES

chapter 17

BUILDING YOUR QueenDOM!

Listen up, my fearless queen! I have got a treat for you, if you are tired of feeling lost and frustrated while trying to set up your business empire. My sassy Business Programs and links are here to rescue you from cluelessness and confusion!

Ever wondered which programs to purchase or which links are actually safe to use? I've got you covered, my queen! Say goodbye to wasting your hard-earned money on useless programs that don't work for you. I've carefully curated a collection of top-notch Business Programs and links just for you. These recommendations are based on intensive research and our own experiences and have saved our company tons of time and money. My goal is to empower you on your journey to build your business empire. Think of it as your personal treasure trove, a roadmap to success. These programs and links have worked wonders for us, and we're confident they'll do the same for you. But remember, you're the one with the power to decide what fits your unique empire-building journey.

Now you can finally take charge, rock that business like the fierce queen you are, and watch those results roll in! So, snatch up our collection of tried-and-true resources, and let's slay this entrepreneurial game together!

STEP 1: Business & Marketing Tools

- **Referral Platform for leads and sales:**
  https://upviral.com/demo/
  An all-round marketing website that helps kickstart your business

- **SEO Check:**
  https://app.neilpatel.com/
  A program to help grow your SEO traffic

- **Zoom Online Meetings:**
  https://zoom.us/
  Online program for video meetings

- **Loom Online Meetings:**
  https://www.loom.com/
  Online program for video meetings

- **DripScripts Email Sequence:**
  https://dripscripts.growthtools.com/signin
  DripScripts lets you customize proven email sequences that are specifically structured to turn leads into customers.

- **Send Files:**
  https://send-anywhere.com/
  A file transferring website that can be used between any other file sharing application

- **Bitly - Shorten your URL Links:**
  https://bitly.com/
  A tool to help shorten your URLs

- **Add Creation:**
  https://adespresso.com/e-commerce/
  A tool that lets you create, analyze And edit your marketing campaigns

- **Audio Transcription:**
  https://www.rev.com/transcription
  In addition to converting your audio & video to text files, this website offers a complete online experience. Transcripts are delivered with powerful tools for interviews, meetings, films, and more.

- **Speech to Text Transcription:**
  https://www.temi.com/
  A website for Speech to text transcription in 5 minutes, advanced speech recognition software.

- **Online Scheduling Assistant:**
  https://bit.ly/3yLrxcT
  A website that acts as your own personal assistant and helps you create schedules for anything you may need.

- **Sales and digital promotions:**
  https://www.clickbank.com/
  ClickBank is a hub for the world's best marketers and most innovative product owners to build businesses that matter.

- **PDF Converter/Compressor:**
  https://smallpdf.com/
  A website that gives you all the tools you'll need to be more productive and work smarter with documents.

- **Advertising and Digital Ads:**
  https://heyhumming.com/
  Humming is the easiest way to manage your advertising, wherever your customers are.

STEP 2: Design

- **Google Fonts:**
  https:fonts.google.com
  Easy access to hundreds of different fonts

- **Free photo image compressor:**
  https://imagecompressor.com/
  This online image optimizer uses a smart combination of the best optimization and lossy compression algorithms to shrink JPEG and PNG images to the minimum possible size while keeping the required level of quality.

- **Making/Editing 3D Clothes:**
  https://www.marvelousdesigner.com/
  Cloth making website for digital artists

- **Psychology of Colors:**
  https://www.empower-yourself-with-color-psychology.com/color-meanings-in-business.html
  A website that teaches you all about the psychology of colors

- **Mock-Ups for advertising:**
  https://smartmockups.com/
  Create professional mockups right inside your browser, even on the go

- **Video Maker:**
  https://wave.video/
  Easily create and edit videos for your social media, emails, website, and blog with just one awesome tool.

- **Easy Video Creation:**
  https://bit.ly/3zMZiMc
  Enjoy exclusive editing styles, full access to iStock media, and customizable colors and fonts. Creating amazing videos is easy. Try Magisto smart video editor for free.

- **E-Book Creation:**
  https://go2.designrr.io
  Create Stunning eBooks & Reports in 2 Minutes Without Writing a Word

- **General Design Creation:**
  https://www.canva.com/
  Online design tool that lets you create whatever you need from thousands of templates

- **Video Editing:**
  https://www.blackmagicdesign.com/products/davinciresolve/
  DaVinci Resolve is the world's only solution that combines editing, color correction, visual effects, motion graphics and audio post-production all in one software tool.

- **Online Flipbook Creation:**
  https://bit.ly/38GEuu7
  Create, share and embed online page flip catalogs, transforming your PDFs into online flipping books. Make a flip book online using our advanced flip book maker. It's free to try.

- **PNG Photo Optimization:**
  https://tinypng.com/
  TinyPNG uses smart lossy compression techniques to reduce the file size of your WEBP, JPEG and PNG files.

- **Remove Image Backgrounds:**
  https://www.remove.bg/
  Remove backgrounds 100% automatically in 5 seconds with zero clicks

- **Mockup & Logo Designs:**
  https://placeit.net/
  A website used to create designs, logos, videos and more in one place

- **Banner Ads & Graphic Design:**
  https://www.20dollarbanners.com/
  A website used to create online add banners for promotion of your business

- **Background and Photo Editing:**
  https://www9.lunapic.com/editor/
  A free online photo editing software

STEP 3: *Engagement*

- **Instagram Engagement Calculator:**
  https://phlanx.com/engagement-calculator
  A website that lets you calculate your engagement rate on Instagram.

- **Analytical tracker for statistics for social media platforms:**
  https://socialblade.com/
  Social Blade tracks user statistics for YouTube, Twitch, Instagram, and Twitter. Get a deeper understanding of user growth and trends by utilizing this website.

- **Website tracking:**
  https://www.similarweb.com/
  Access behind-the-scenes analytics for every site online. With the Similarweb TrafficMeter™ browser extension, you'll have easy access to objective traffic data and other insights, as you surf.

- **Learn How to Create Funnels:**
  https://cfdesignschool.com/
  Free online funnel training program.

STEP 4: *Social Media*

- **QR Code generator:**
  https://bit.ly/3tj8jdA
  QRCode Monkey is one of the most popular free online QR code generators with millions of already created QR codes. Can be used for commercial and print purposes.

- **Online Streaming:**
  https://streamyard.com/pricing
  Website to create live streams

- **Performance Content:**
  https://viralfindr.com/
  ViralFindr is a simpler way to find the best performing content on Instagram. Use it for inspiration to create your own or download to ANY device and repost to your feed.

- **Paid Influencers for Shoutouts:**
  https://shoutcart.com/
  A website that helps connect you with popular influencers to get your brand in front of their audience.

- **One Page Social Media:**
  https://onespotsocial.com/
  One Spot Social is the easiest way to create a personal page that showcases which social networks you use.

- **Instagram Automation:**
  https://izood.net/pricing
  Website that can grant you access to different automation streams for different apps like Instagram or YouTube,

- **Video Sharing:**
  https://vimeo.com/upgrade
  Online platform for sharing video content

- **Music for online promo:**
  https://bit.ly/3zPIYu3
  An online music library with royalty-free music that can be used for videos or other creative projects

Sassy Lips

STEP 5: *Legal*

- **Company and Trademark Registration:**
  https://legalvision.grsm.io/armanagement
  A website that lets you register your business trademark

- **Professional Legal advice:**
  https://legalvision.com.au/
  An online legal website that links you with real professionals to take care of the legal side of your business

- **Business forms & Documents:**
  https://www.lawdepot.com/
  A free website that provides you with templates to hundreds of documents for business and personal use.

- **Legal Online Services:**
  https://sprintlaw.com.au/services/
  A website with 100+ legal service packages

STEP 6: *Online Accounting Programs*

- **Quickbooks:**
  https://quickbooks.intuit.com/au
  An online accounting program for small businesses

- **Xero:**
  https://www.xero.com/au
  An online accounting software for your business, connects you to your bank, accountant, bookkeeper, and other business apps.

QuickBooks is best for businesses that require desktop accounting software and outsource their accounting tasks to a bookkeeper or accountant, while Xero is a better fit for businesses that need online accounting software and unlimited users.

STEP 7: *How to use the above links and programs*

- First and foremost, take a moment to acknowledge the significance of this opportunity. You now hold in your hands a powerful arsenal of knowledge, strategies, and tools that have the potential to transform your business and your life.

- Embrace this moment with gratitude and excitement, knowing that you are taking a significant step towards manifesting your dreams. As you explore each program and link, approach it with an open mind and a willingness to learn.

- Read through their offerings, watch video tutorials, and immerse yourself in the content they provide. These resources have been carefully curated to equip you with the skills and insights needed to navigate the entrepreneurial world with confidence.

- Take some time to familiarize yourself with each program and link. Read through their offerings, watch tutorials, and understand how they can benefit your business. Identify which aspects of your business you want to focus on first, whether it's developing a solid business plan, refining your branding, or mastering marketing strategies.

- Create a step-by-step action plan based on your priorities. Set specific goals and deadlines for each task you want to accomplish. Having a clear roadmap will keep you organized and focused as you move forward.

- Don't hesitate to immerse yourself in learning and take advantage of the resources provided, my queen. Attend webinars, participate in workshops, and engage with the online communities associated with these programs. These opportunities will provide valuable insights and connect you with like-minded individuals who can offer support and advice.

- As you embark on this journey, remember that progress may not always be linear, and that's okay. Celebrate your successes, no matter how small, and learn from any challenges or setbacks. Stay persistent and committed to your vision.

- Most importantly, keep your passion alive, my queen. Your business is a reflection of your dreams and aspirations, and your unwavering belief in your vision will drive you forward even during tough times. Trust in yourself and the value you bring to the world through your business.

SPECIAL INVITATION

To My Queen:

As I sit down to write these words,
I can't help but feel the surge of excitement
that comes with inviting you to embark on a
journey that has the potential to change your
life forever.

Sassy Lips

Imagine for a moment that you're standing at the threshold of your dreams — a realm where your aspirations bloom into a breathtaking reality. Can you feel it? Your heart is racing, your spirit is ignited — this is your kingdom, waiting for you to claim it.

I know how it feels to wonder whether your dreams are attainable, whether you can truly step into your power. Let me reassure you, there's no coincidence that you're reading these words right now. This very moment has a purpose, and you're meant to be here. Your potential is limitless, and here you are at this crucial point — a defining moment to choose between the uncertainties that linger and the powerful pull of your dreams.

Right now, you stand at a crossroads — a pivotal moment that holds the power to shape the trajectory of your dreams. The choice before you is simple, yet profound: to say YES or to let this opportunity slip away. I want you to pause for a moment and imagine what it would feel like to take that leap of faith and embrace your dreams with unwavering determination.

I want to remind you that barriers and challenges are a natural part of any journey. They are not roadblocks but stepping stones, guiding you towards the opportunities that await you. I encourage you to look beyond the obstacles and envision the limitless potential that lies ahead. You are more than capable of overcoming anything that stands in your way.

Imagine your story becoming the cornerstone of an empire — a story that resonates with hearts, ignites sparks of inspiration, and beckons investments from those who see your brilliance. Building a business goes beyond profits; it's about crafting a legacy that leaves an indelible mark.

Let me share a glimpse of my own journey with you. Just like you, I once stood at a similar crossroads, torn between doubts and aspirations. I know what it's like to face adversity, to navigate through uncharted territory, and to ultimately find my way to a place where I am doing what I love and loving what I do. And now, I want to be your guide, your partner on this incredible expedition.

Imagine having someone by your side who understands what it's like to be in your shoes, someone who has not only walked the talk but has triumphed over challenges. I want to be that guiding light for you, to share my insights, experiences, and wisdom as you venture towards your dreams.

As your potential business coach, I see the fire within you — the same fire that has fueled my own journey. I believe that your dreams are worth pursuing, and I'm here to help you uncover the path that leads to your aspirations. Together, we can navigate through

Sassy Lips

the uncertainties, overcome obstacles, and create a roadmap to success.

So, my queen, the time has come to make a choice that could lead you to new heights. Saying YES may be the turning point that propels you towards a life filled with purpose, fulfillment, and achievement. I invite you to consider this as an opportunity — an opportunity for growth, for transformation, and for realizing the dreams that have been residing in your heart.

If you're ready to take that step, if you're prepared to say YES to your dreams, I am here, eager and honored to join you on this journey as your business coach. Let's explore the endless possibilities that lie ahead, break down barriers, and carve a path towards your dream destination.

To take the first step towards this incredible journey of transformation, simply reach out to me via email at **contact@aroharipley.com** or visit my website **aroharipley.com/fearlessqueens**.

I can't wait to connect with you, hear your aspirations, and help you unlock the doors to your dreams. Let's embark on this exciting path together, my queen!

Here's to conquering dreams, breaking barriers, and celebrating every triumph together.

With unstoppable determination and love,

your Sassy and Fearless Queen *Aroha*

MY PRAYER for
SASSY LIPS FEARLESS QUEENS

Dear Heavenly Father ...

Sassy Lips

Today, I come before you with a heart filled with love and gratitude for the incredible queens you have placed in my life. I lift them up in prayer, seeking your divine guidance and encouragement as they journey through life's challenges and pursue their dreams.

I ask you to surround our queens with your boundless love and strength. Fill them with courage and determination to face every obstacle that comes their way. Grant them the wisdom to discern the right path and the perseverance to overcome any doubts or fears that may try to hold them back.

May they always know their worth and recognize the incredible potential within them. Let them be reminded that they are fearfully and wonderfully made, uniquely designed with gifts and talents that have the power to impact the world.

Heavenly Father, I pray that you ignite a fire within our queens, a passion that drives them to seek greatness and make a difference in the lives of others. Grant them the grace to embrace their true selves, to walk boldly in their purpose, and to lead with compassion and humility.

In moments of uncertainty, I ask for your gentle touch to soothe their hearts and calm their minds. Remind them that you are always by their side, guiding and supporting them each step of the way. Let them find solace in your presence and draw strength from your unfailing love.

I pray that you surround our queens with a community of support and encouragement. Bless them with genuine friendships and mentors who lift them up, inspire them, and help them grow.

Help them see the beauty and potential in every situation, even amidst challenges and setbacks. May they find the silver linings in adversity and use them as stepping stones to reach higher heights.

Above all, Jesus, I pray that our queens never lose sight of their dreams. May you awaken their dreams and visions within, and may they have the courage to pursue their aspirations with unwavering faith, knowing that with you, all things are possible. May they realize that you want them to succeed in every area of their lives and that success is a good thing when you are at the helm and can be enjoyed by all.

May they find joy in the journey and embrace every opportunity for growth and transformation. May they be filled with your love in all that they do, knowing that their future is bright and that you have a purpose and a plan for their lives. May they come to know you Jesus as their personal Saviour just as I have, and may they find peace and fulfilment in all that they do.

Sassy Lips

I thank you, Heavenly Father, for the incredible queens you have placed in our lives. I pray that you continue to bless and protect them, guide and inspire them, and shower them with your abundant love, grace, and favor.

In your precious name, I pray,

Amen.

ABOUT THE AUTHOR

Aroha Ripley is of Māori descent, and a true inspiration, hailing from the beautiful land of Aotearoa, New Zealand, born in Whakatane and raised in the small towns of Levin and Hawera before making her mark in Brisbane, Australia. Aroha wears many hats — she's a devoted wife, a loving mother, and a doting nanny. But above all, her heart is anchored in her family, her unwavering love for God, and her heart's desire to serve people with love and encouragement to fulfill their life's purpose.

Aroha's life has been a testament to the power of resilience and the beauty that can arise from ashes. Her journey of triumph over adversity has fueled her with a mission to fearlessly speak to women who might feel powerless in the face of challenges, yet harbor dreams that refuse to be silenced. With an unshakable belief in unlocking the potential for beauty from even the toughest trials, Aroha empowers women to rise above their obstacles and embrace their divine calling.

She's a firestarter, igniting the entrepreneurial spirit within others, encouraging them to boldly step into their dreams and claim their throne of greatness. Aroha's confidence and boldness inspire women to shine as queens and fearlessly show the world their unapologetic greatness.

Aroha's passion lies in helping women embrace their unique life stories and transform them into messages of hope. She stands as a beacon of light for those who have faced brokenness, urging them to seize every opportunity life presents and step into their queendom. Her story is a testament to the power of embracing life and finding the silver linings in every situation. From Aroha's incredible life journey emerged the empowering book *Sassy Lips, Fearless Queens*.

As a business and life coach, Aroha fearlessly encourages women to speak with boldness and authority. Her mission is to ignite the fire within them, inspiring them to rise, embrace their true calling, and fearlessly step into their destined greatness. With Aroha's guidance and support, women are empowered to unleash their inner power and confidently pursue their dreams.

ACKNOWLEDGMENTS

First of all, I want to thank my Lord Jesus for awakening my spirit within and for giving me the love, courage, and strength to write for my queens, for the inspiration, and for the creative ideas you have placed in my heart. I truly give you all the glory and praise. To my first ever business coach, Tracy Wilson: I will be forever grateful for our first meeting back in 2019, where my journey began to become an entrepreneur in business. The invitation to travel with you and John for nine weeks to America and to travel to eight states to learn from amazing business owners and entrepreneurs was an opportunity that set my life on an amazing journey of success and continues today. I will forever be grateful to you.

Sassy Lips

To Rebekah Robinson, thank you for your amazing graphic design in formatting my book to prepare my masterpiece for publishing and for introducing me to my first ever editor, Anne.

To Anne Hamilton, thank you for your amazing insight and professionalism as an editor in making my book *Sassy Lips, Fearless Queens* flow and sound with such impact.

To the numerous and blessed friends I have — too many to name — who have kept me in prayer and supported me throughout this process of writing my first ever book. I pray God's love and unmerited favor continue to shine upon you. I love you all.

To the amazing people and business entrepreneurs who have endorsed my book *Sassy Lips, Fearless Queens*, thank you from the bottom of my heart. Your support and kind words have been instrumental in sharing the book's message and empowering women to fulfill their dreams. I am truly grateful for our collaboration and excited for the future.

Finally, to my loving husband, Darrin, I am beyond grateful for the love and strength you've poured into my life throughout this incredible journey. Your unwavering support, patience, and understanding have been the cornerstones of my success. From late nights to long days, you've been there with cups of tea and coffee, meals served with a smile or a laugh, reminding me that I'm not alone in this pursuit. Your creative input has added a special touch to my work, and I cherish every moment we share. I love you more than words can express, my honey.

To my amazing children Romaine, Janaya, and Jesse, and my caring daughters-in-law Ema and Nina, and our precious *Mokos*, Eva, Isla, Willow, Wynter and our beautiful angel Melody — you are the light of my life, and your love sustains me every day. Your love and encouragement have been a driving force behind this endeavor, and I am deeply grateful for the laughter and joy you bring into my world. Without your unwavering support and feedback, this book would not have been possible. You are my heart and soul, and I feel truly blessed to have you as my family.

I want each of you to know that you hold a special place in my heart, and I pray that you will be encouraged to chase after your dreams with unyielding determination. Your potential knows no bounds, and I have no doubt that you will achieve greatness in whatever you set your mind to. Remember, I will always be here to cheer you on and offer my unwavering love, prayer and support. Love you always *Mum xx*

WANT TO KNOW MORE?

Aroha is the Founder and Director of AR Personal Artist Management, a multifaceted platform offering an array of services encompassing Business Coaching, Online Education Courses, Workshops, and Website Design and Development. Aroha has worked with international, national, and local businesses. Drawing from her extensive expertise, Aroha specializes in guiding women through the transformative journey from traditional 9-to-5 roles to the dynamic landscape of entrepreneurship, leveraging their unique life stories as catalysts for business success.

With a wide-ranging clientele that spans industries such as commercial real estate, life coaching, counseling, homemaking, beauty, fashion, resilience coaching, and the creative arts, Aroha's professional demeanor and wealth of knowledge make her a standout figure. Renowned for her unwavering commitment to integrity and an unstinting work ethic, she consistently goes above and beyond to deliver exceptional results for her clients.

Aroha's dedication has given birth to something truly special. She's created a space where women's voices echo, hearts mend, and purposes reignite. Guided by Aroha's own spirit, women from all walks of life set forth on a journey of self-discovery, uncovering their individual paths and embracing their callings. And that's how the *Sassy Lips, Fearless Queens* empire came to be — a living tribute to the collective might of women. Driven by a shared determination to conquer hurdles, they celebrated their openness and authenticity. This journey isn't just about facing challenges; it's about celebrating victories, rekindling inner strength, and awakening dreams that may have laid dormant.

At the center of it all, Aroha shines as a guiding star — an agent of change and a source of hope. As lives transform, the Fearless Queens empire grows into a testament of the remarkable power of women uniting, reclaiming their strength, and crafting unique paths in this vast world.

To find out more about Aroha's services or products, including her written works, comprehensive programs, immersive workshops, and upcoming events, please explore **www.aroharipley.com**.

For inquiries regarding bookings or collaborative opportunities, don't hesitate to reach out via email at **contact@aroharipley.com**. Additionally, you can connect directly with Aroha through various social media platforms.

www.aroharipley.com

www.ingramcontent.com/pod-product-compliance
Lightning Source LLC
Chambersburg PA
CBHW051426290426
44109CB00016B/1444